THE FIRST
CHRISTMAS
CAROL

A MISER, A MANGER, A MIRACLE

MARIANNE JORDAN

D0104991

Lighthouse Publishing
of the Carolinas

www.lighthousepublishingofthecarolinas.com

THE FIRST CHRISTMAS CAROL - A MISER, A MANGER, A
MIRACLE BY MARIANNE JORDAN
Published by Lighthouse Publishing of the Carolinas
2333 Barton Oaks Dr., Raleigh, NC, 27614

ISBN 978-1938499739
Copyright © 2013 by Marianne Jordan
Cover design by Urosh Bizjak, uroshb.prosite.com and
Ted Ruybal, www.wisdomhousebooks.com
Book design by The Fast Fingers, www.thefastfingers.com

Available in print from your local bookstore, online, or from the publisher
at: www.lighthousepublishingofthecarolinas.com

For more information on this author,
visit: https:www.facebook.com/AuthorMarianneJordan

Brought to you by the creative team at
LighthousePublishingoftheCarolinas.com:
Eddie Jones, Elizabeth Easter, Brian Cross, and Rowena Kuo.

Library of Congress Cataloging-in-Publication Data
Jordan, Marianne.
The First Christmas Carol - a miser, a manger, a miracle / Marianne Jordan
1st ed.

Printed in the United States of America

Dedication

For Mason, the gift that keeps on giving.

Acknowledgments

I owe so many people my gratitude that I find it difficult to know where to begin.

I originally wrote *The First Christmas Carol* in 1999 as a play for the church youth drama team, Rubicon. They were an extraordinary group of kids, and it was because of them, and all those associated with those performances at New Horizons Fellowship, that the story was born. I still have the cast picture on my bookshelf and the program in a frame. Those wonderful people changed my life.

Years later, I attended my first Blue Ridge Mountain Writers Conference. I had no idea what I was doing, but an agent liked my idea and decided to take me on. I used to dream of being able to publicly thank you, Jonathan Clements, for seeing past the inexperience and undeveloped talent. You took a risk, Jonathan. I'm forever grateful. I'd never have gotten this far without you. I hope our journey is just beginning.

I owe more gratitude to Eddie Jones and Lighthouse Publishing of the Carolinas than I know how to express. It wasn't easy, I know, but through your guidance and patience, I'm living my dream. I'm also checking into buying us some stock in Panera Bread, and season tickets to the Durham Bulls in 2014.

Elizabeth Easter, you deserve a gold medal for your gift and talent for editing, and another one for patience. Thank you, Elizabeth. Maybe now I'll know when to use an em dash and an ellipsis.

I also want to recognize Rowena Kuo, Acquisitions Editor and Editorial Director for Lighthouse Publishing. I probably owe you several towels and bottles of vitamin water. Not only did you rush to make our deadline, you had to teach me the ropes. Thank you.

There are many friends and family members who've encouraged me, pushed me, and wondered if I'd ever follow through with writing a book. You believed long before I did. Thank you.

Jessica and Bill, there are no words. The dictionary and thesaurus come up empty. *I love you* doesn't come close. Just know I do. With all my heart.

One

If only he weren't dead.

Standing in the entrance to the inn, Ebenezer watched the chaos in the square. The crowd scattered in every direction as the Roman soldiers on horseback stampeded through the market. To avoid being trampled, some people tried to shove by the innkeeper seeking cover, but Ebenezer didn't budge.

"They don't pass through this door unless they're prepared to pay!" he sneered.

Ebenezer began to laugh, but immediately doubled over in a coughing fit that rattled his insides. The dust kicked up by the horses irritated his eyes and coated his throat, making it difficult to catch his breath. His eyes burned with salty tears. He hacked up milky phlegm and spit it on the ground. Finally, he stopped wheezing and wiped his face with the back of his hand.

Resting his shoulder against the doorpost, he said softly, "Oh, Jacob, how you would have loved this. Look at them all. Hundreds lining up to register, and each needing a place to eat and sleep. Well, come, come, you weary souls, for I have room

1

and will gladly give you rest." A contemptuous smile parted his wiry beard. "Gladly, that is, after I deplete you of everything in your purse. Provided Caesar leaves you anything!"

Ebenezer was right. His former business partner would have loved the delightful sounds of potential profit as tired, anxious travelers filtered into Bethlehem. Loved it as much as he. Ebenezer scoffed.

If he weren't dead.

Two

Ebenezer turned and stepped through the doorway, his elbow brushing against the mezuzah hanging on the frame. Like the one at his home, it had been a fixture of the inn since its construction. And like the one in his home, the mezuzah was severely cracked and chipped. It was amazing it remained attached at all. Ebenezer refused to fix either. To repair them would have been an unnecessary expense.

Most Jews who came through the door automatically reached to kiss the small scripture casing, only to find pieces crumble in their hands. Ebenezer had all but forgotten it was even there, but now the disintegrating symbol caught his attention. The small indentation appeared to be the image of a woman's face.

Was that—? No, it couldn't be.

He squeezed his eyes and shook his head, slinging drops of sweat around him. When he looked again, the silhouette had disappeared. He tilted closer, running his fingers over the fissures. *Impossible.*

With a cursing grunt, he whirled and plowed into his assistant, Aaron.

"Why don't you look where you're going?" Ebenezer bellowed.

The crowd waiting in the reception area quieted. The lull was brief. Nobody cared.

"But you were the one who—"

"Any rooms left?" snapped Ebenezer, cutting him off.

"Only one."

"Excellent. Make sure you fill every space of the building, including the roof and outside walls. If anyone is sitting, lying, or leaning against even an inch of this inn, they are to pay for it, understood?"

"Yes, but if I am tending to the guests, you cannot possibly expect me to—"

"There are others, maybe even some here"—Ebenezer surveyed the crowded room—"who would be pleased to have room, board, *and* employment."

Aaron took a deep breath and eyed Ebenezer. For a moment the younger man appeared as though he might respond. Ebenezer silently hoped he would. How he loved putting others in their place.

"Excuse me. Would you happen to be the proprietor of this inn?"

Ebenezer whirled, and quickly sized up the gentlemen in his doorway. By their dress, they were men of means and rank. He glowered at Aaron. He had no intention of letting these guests deal with his lowly assistant. They were obviously used to dealing with those prominent in the business world. Aaron unobtrusively moved out of the way.

"I am Ebenezer, the owner of this inn. Are you in need of accommodations?"

"We will need a room."

"Yes, yes, of course. As I was explaining to my assistant, we have only one room left. I am sure it will suit your needs. You will be most comfortable there."

The man who'd asked the question was short and heavy. He wore expensive rings on several fingers. Ebenezer took this as a good sign. The taller man had a neatly trimmed beard and bushy eyebrows, and his stylish outer garment was clasped together by a jeweled gold broach, but Ebenezer didn't care to converse with him. He was slightly taller than Ebenezer, so the innkeeper merely nodded at the gentleman. To look at him directly would require Ebenezer to look up at the man, and he hated looking up to anybody.

"The room is not for us," the second man explained. "We are here on behalf of those who have nowhere else to go and cannot afford the high rates charged by—"

Ebenezer lifted one eyebrow. *They want charity? From me?*

Struggling to keep calm, he replied, "We are full." He turned to go back to his private room.

The first man spoke as if he hadn't heard a word Ebenezer said. "The taxes of Rome have placed an unnecessary burden on our people. This census alone is proof of that. Would you turn away your neighbors?"

"I have no neighbors."

"Very well, perhaps you would consider donating funds to help those less fortunate."

"I would not. What I *would like* is to be left alone. I pay my taxes. Taxes that help pay for debtors' prisons where the so-called 'less fortunate' can go."

"Many would rather die than see their families in such places."

At this, Ebenezer all but lunged forward, coming to stand with his face only inches from the generous man. "If the poor refuse to avail themselves of the free room and board offered in such places, what business is that of mine? If they choose to die, so be it. There will be less population to feed. It doesn't matter to me. They can sleep in the streets, for all I care. Just keep them away from my door! Now then, you are wasting my time. Good day, gentlemen."

The thin man took a step forward, his black brows furrowed in anger. "You might not be so unfeeling if you paid a little more attention to those around you and the way they are forced to live."

Ebenezer's anger made him mentally lord over the taller guest. "That would require putting my nose in other people's business," he hissed. "I make it a point to never get involved in other people's business."

He held his ground, his glare shifting between the two men. Without a word, the pair pivoted and left.

When they were out of earshot, Ebenezer turned to the customers still gathered around the table where Aaron sat with the ledger of occupants. "Aaron, would you *please* take these people's money and get them out of here?"

Three

Ebenezer was relieved to be in the sanctuary of his private room. It had been a long, trying day. Profitable, but exhausting. The sun would be setting soon, and Aaron had started lighting the lamps. Out in the main room, the smell of the oil mixed with body odors, stale wine, and animal dung was overwhelming. He'd even seen a woman vomit in the corner of the room. He made Aaron scoop up the mess then cover the dirt floor with a thin layer of straw picked up from elsewhere in the room. The rancid air was stifling.

Ebenezer's head throbbed. Maybe he'd lie down on the worn cushions scattered around the room and rest. Better yet, he went behind a large, scarred, splintered wooden table and pulled out the new wineskin from a hidden shelf.

He had no problem reusing the old skins for the watered-down wine he served patrons. Only a few might notice the difference, so he saw no reason to spend the money.

This, however, was a fine wine he'd purchased on a recent trip to Jerusalem, and one not to be shared with just anyone. No. He reserved this for his own personal consumption, and for those who had status or the means to make a profitable business deal.

Looking around, he realized he'd forgotten his goblet. Growling at having to return to the public room filled with sweating, filthy commoners, Ebenezer gave a quick thought to drinking straight from the skin. This seemed a shameful disrespect, however, an irreverent gesture to such an expensive wine. So, hauling himself out of the chair, he prepared for the putrid odor about to assault his senses.

Swinging open the door, he came face-to-face with his nephew, Isaac.

"What do you want?" Ebenezer shoved his way past the young man, his gaze darting around the room in search of his expensive chalice.

It was wall-to-wall people, and finding anything was going to be difficult. A cup would be nearly impossible to locate. Squatting down, all Ebenezer could see were the dirty, frayed hems of scratchy robes and filthy sandaled feet. With so much shuffling and dragging of tired legs, moldy straw was bunched in tiny mounds, as if a rodent had burrowed through the room. Ebenezer stood on his tip-toes, but that didn't help. It was like standing in a grove of olive trees on a breezy day. Human trunks with swaying heads and arms. The smoke from burning lamps clouded the room, and did nothing to aid in his search.

"Uncle, I've come to ask—"

"If it's about my joining you and your wife for the Sabbath celebration, forget it." Ebenezer swept Aaron's organized ledgers onto the dirt floor as he continued to forage the desk for his favorite goblet. "Go right ahead, if you have that much time to squander, but I'll not lose income while I sit in the synagogue listening to old men read from the Torah."

"Receiving God's law into one's heart is *not* squandering time."

"Is to me. If the Almighty wants to speak to *my* heart, He needs to rethink His schedule. Now, out of my way."

At that moment, Ebenezer spotted his precious goblet underneath a small, low table near the doorway. Easily accessible when watching the crowd but not where patrons would normally look. Ebenezer hesitated, remembering the face in the mezuzah. He wasn't sure he wanted to go near it.

Pointing, he ordered Isaac to retrieve the gold cup.

When Ebenezer reached for it, Isaac grabbed his uncle's sleeve and pulled him close so that only the two could hear. "I want nothing from you, ask nothing of you. I simply want to spend time together as family. Whether you choose to acknowledge it or not, your blood flows within me."

Ebenezer yanked his arm away. He hissed, "Leave me alone."

"I do not know what I did to displease you."

"You were born!" His voice reverberated throughout the room.

The din of conversation and emotional exchange fell silent, every eye turned toward the two men. Anger reddened Ebenezer's face, and his breathing labored.

For a moment, no one moved.

Backing away, Isaac gave a slight bow to his uncle and turned to Aaron. "God's peace to you and your family."

"And to you and yours."

The room was still quiet. Ebenezer looked around. "There's nothing here to look at! Go about your business!"

The crowd resumed its complaining, arguing, and worrying. People had their own problems, and the crazed innkeeper wasn't one of them.

Ebenezer watched his nephew pause outside the front door, waiting as more Roman soldiers marched past. Beyond the forest of legs he noticed a small boy splayed out on the ground, a crutch beside him.

Ebenezer turned on his assistant. "I am not paying you to just stand around and breathe. Get back to work. I want this inn full! Not a centimeter unoccupied. And every shekel accounted for. Do you understand?"

Aaron nodded.

With his precious goblet in hand, Ebenezer returned to his private room. He sampled the new wine, savoring its sweetness. As he did, a memory came to him, one he hadn't recalled for a very long time—a saying told to him by his father when Ebenezer was but a boy: "If you put new wine in old wine skins, you will lose both the wine and the skin, Ebe."

Ebenezer had not understood his father's words.

"You will, Ebe. When you are old, like me, you will."

Old, set in my ways. "And rich because of it," he muttered as he filled his cup once more. He took no time to enjoy the taste. He guzzled it.

Red wine splashed onto his outer robe, but he didn't care. He wiped his whiskered mouth with his sleeve.

Closing his eyes, he tried to tamp down his anger, but instead a mental image of Isaac interrupted his thoughts. His nephew was a pestering fly that needed to be squashed. Isaac's weekly visits had become increasingly disruptive, and it was time to put an end to them. First, however, Ebenezer needed to focus on the crowd descending on Bethlehem, and how he could exploit the situation. He would deal with Isaac later.

Stretching, Ebenezer looked around the room. Unlike the outer room, Ebenezer's private area had a stone floor, covered with a carpet. At one time, it had been beautiful, but like the cushions, the colors had long faded, and the edges were torn and frayed. It was covered with stains, especially around his table where he haphazardly dropped food and spilled wine. Ebenezer stared at the empty goblet. He had another at home that was even more beautiful.

He sighed. "Home."

Maybe that's what he should do. Go home. He could just as

easily work there, and he wouldn't have to deal with the noise and stench coming from the inn's common area.

Ebenezer stacked his ledgers on the table. They were heavy, but it didn't matter. They were filled with financial transactions. Lines of numbers that added up to hefty profits. He'd carry them anywhere.

Four

aron couldn't remember when he'd ever been this hot or as tired. All he wanted to do was go home, pour a jar of cool water over his head, then lie down and sleep for three days.

The room was packed. Not just with people and their belongings, but with tension—an invisible entity hanging heavy overhead. It was smothering. Like sheep corralled in a small pen, people stepped on one another, jabbed each other with elbows, or accidentally punched someone in the face. There was a cacophony of noise, and Aaron had to shout to be heard. Patience was in short supply, and tempers flared.

Ebenezer, on the other hand, would be thrilled. There was only one room left, and it would only go to someone who could afford to pay the exorbitant fee. The rest of the inn was full. Not one inch of wall or floor space left.

The crowd shifted, and Aaron looked up. His family came through the doorway, his youngest son, Timothy, leading the way. When people noticed the boy, they tried to make room for him.

Timothy had been born a cripple. His left leg was twisted, his foot deformed. He'd never been able to walk without aid.

13

A sickly child often confined to the bed, he never complained. Even now, as he struggled to maneuver on his small crutch, Timothy greeted his father with a huge smile.

Aaron hurried around the table and swept his tiny son into his arms. "What are you doing here?" He kissed the boy on both cheeks.

"We came to help you!" Timothy's large brown eyes twinkled with excitement.

Martha came to stand by her husband. Though right next to him, she had to raise her voice. "We brought you dinner. I wasn't sure if you'd eaten today. By the looks of things, it would be safe to surmise you haven't." She looked around. "I imagine Ebenezer's quite pleased."

"He will be." Aaron handed Timothy to his oldest son. "Listen, Martha, I appreciate the food, but I think you need to leave."

"What? Why? We can help you."

"Actually, it would help me more if you'd go. Ebenezer is in a terrible mood, and I don't want to cause any more trouble. I'm not sure how he'd react if he saw you here."

"I don't understand. Why in the world would he be in a foul mood? Look at this place! He's making money. That's the *one thing* that makes the man happy."

"He had a run-in with some gentlemen who wanted a free room or financial donation to a charity fund. I'm sure you can imagine how that turned out. And then he had another visit from his nephew."

Aaron paused long enough to answer a guest's question, then turned his attention back to his wife.

"I still can't believe he wants nothing to do with the boy." Martha shook her head. "Isaac is his only living relative. They're family!"

"Don't remind Ebenezer of that. First, Isaac isn't a boy. He's a grown man. A man Ebenezer sees as a murderer and a thief."

"You've never told me that—you just said they don't get along. Why would Ebenezer think such a thing?"

"Ebenezer was very close to his sister. From what I gather, she was the only person he's ever loved more than himself. She died in childbirth, and he holds Isaac responsible."

Aaron stepped aside and took care of another guest. Martha told the children they needed to wait for her outside. This was met with disgruntled faces and audible exasperation. Martha reminded them of their place and shooed them from the room.

Aaron stood beside her again.

"Why would Ebenezer think Isaac's a thief?"

"Because he believes Isaac only wants to get on his good side so he can inherit the inn." He looked around to make sure the innkeeper was nowhere in sight. "Martha, I appreciate what you're trying to do, but please. Take the children and go home. I don't want Ebenezer taking out his anger on you and the family."

Their presence could also cost Aaron his job, but he didn't say that to Martha.

She studied her husband. "All right. We'll go. But only because you're telling us to. I still think we could do some good here."

"I'm sure you could. It's just not the right time."

"Do you know when you're coming home?"

"No, but you know where to find me should you need me."

Aaron didn't have to say more. He knew Martha understood he was referring to Timothy. They'd had these implied conversations before.

"I'll see you soon." Martha leaned as close to Aaron's ear as she could. "I love you."

He touched his wife's cheek, and she turned to go.

"Martha?"

She turned around.

Aaron held out his hand. "The food?"

His wife laughed. "Oh, yes. I'm sorry. Here." She handed him the small bundle. "I'm a little distracted." She looked around the room. "I guess everyone is." She shrugged, and gave her husband a parting smile. "See you soon."

Aaron watched her leave.

It couldn't have been easy for her to come to the inn today. Or any day, for that matter. Martha struggled with anger and resentment in her heart toward Ebenezer. She had no use for him. She only allowed his name mentioned inside their home because he was Aaron's employer. Martha tried to pray for Ebenezer, but it always turned into a prayer for Aaron to find another job so he could get out from under the weight of working for such a greedy, cruel, odious man. She found it ironic that the name Ebenezer meant *stone of help*. To Martha, it meant *heart of stone*.

While no one seemed to need his immediate attention, Aaron opened the bundle. He hadn't eaten since morning and was famished. He discreetly said a blessing and began to eat. While savoring Martha's cooking, Aaron thought about his family. Especially Timothy. He was much smaller than other children his age, and doctors gave little hope he would grow much more. In fact, they gave little hope he'd grow at all. They'd told Martha and Aaron that Timothy would most likely die within a year. He just wasn't strong enough to withstand the illness ravishing his diminutive body.

They'd yet to tell the other children about the dark prognosis, but it probably wasn't necessary; though Timothy kept a wonderful attitude, he continued to decline. It was better to maintain the impression that all was well, and hold tightly to the belief that God would create a miracle for Timothy.

Aaron's belief, however, was starting to waver. His child needed a specialist, and there was no way he could afford to pay the cost. Besides, it would require traveling to Jerusalem or even farther, and Ebenezer would never let him take the time off—not if Aaron wanted to keep his job. His hope for a miracle dwindled.

He looked around the room. Each had their own hurts, their own problems to worry about. Why should he be any different? But—

A tired-looking guest was headed toward him, so Aaron wrapped up the rest of his meal and set it aside. *I'm weary, too. Weary and worried.* Yes, why should he be any different?

Five

Some of the lamps were beginning to dim, so Aaron slowly moved around the room, adding a small amount of oil to each. Though it meant he had to do it more often, he intentionally didn't fill them to capacity. The room was much too crowded. It would only take a small amount of oil and flame to set the room ablaze. There would be mass panic and—

He didn't want to even think about it.

There was a commotion at the entrance, and Aaron made his way to the front. Timothy stood in front of the large table, holding a man's hand.

Where was Martha? Why wasn't Timothy with her at home?

Aaron tried to keep his voice level, his frustration contained. "Timothy? Why are you here? You were supposed to be going home. Where is your mother?"

"She's at the well. An old woman needed help drawing water, so Mother's doing it."

Aaron had to bite his lip. "You should have stayed with her."

"I couldn't. I needed to introduce you to Joseph."

The man stepped forward. "I'm sorry. I didn't realize that Timothy wasn't supposed to be here. He said you could help us with a room."

"Joseph saved my life today!" Timothy beamed at the man.

"What? What do you mean he saved your life?" Aaron looked at his son, then the man, then back to his son.

"I didn't save your life, Timothy. I merely moved you out of the way of the horses."

Aaron frowned. His confusion wasn't assuaging his frustration at seeing his son return to the inn. "Let's start at the beginning. What happened?"

Joseph started to answer, but Timothy raced ahead.

"We were on our way to see you, and the soldiers weren't looking where they were going. Joseph pushed me because I couldn't get out of the way fast enough!" Timothy made it sound like an exciting adventure.

Aaron's temper was rising, but he tried to keep it from showing. "And where was your mother?"

"Somebody stopped her to ask for directions. I—" Timothy looked at his father's face, likely realizing he was in trouble. "I didn't wait for her. I know I should have, but we were just across from the inn, and I wanted to see you." Timothy's voice faltered, his bottom lip quivered, and he looked as if he might cry.

Joseph stepped in. "The horses came through so quickly, they took everyone by surprise. I honestly think the soldiers did it deliberately. I believe they enjoy it." He looked down at the crippled child. "I figured a skinned knee was better than the alternative." He tousled Timothy's hair.

Aaron took a deep breath, and slowly exhaled. "Thank you for protecting my boy." He gave Joseph a nod.

Timothy looked up at Aaron. "I'm sorry, Father."

"Son, I know you didn't intentionally do anything wrong, but you can't go off on your own like that. We've talked about it. Until this registration is over, you are to stay with a family member. Understood?"

Timothy looked down at his feet. Aaron's heart melted. He knelt and pulled Timothy into his arms.

"I don't know what I'd do if anything happened to you." Aaron was exhausted, and afraid he'd break down and cry on the spot; one day, he'd have to face that very thing.

"Don't worry, Father. I won't do it again." Timothy hugged Aaron's neck.

Glancing over the child's shoulder, Aaron saw Joseph looking at them, a strange expression on his face.

"Is there something I can do for you?" Aaron stood. "It seems I'm in your debt."

"I told Joseph that you could find them a place to stay," declared Timothy. "Mary's going to have a baby!"

Aaron looked at Joseph. "Mary is your—"

"She's my wife. And, yes, she's pregnant."

There was a long pause. Aaron fumbled with what to say. "I-I'm not sure—"

His robe tightened around his neck. He stumbled as he was pulled backward. *Ebenezer.* Aaron's gut churned.

Ebenezer pulled Aaron out of sight, but it didn't matter. Everyone in the front room could hear him berate his assistant.

"Does that man have any money?"

"I don't know."

"I can tell just by looking at him that he doesn't, so he shouldn't even be inside these walls. I told you, no one comes through that door for any reason unless they have money in hand. Get him out of here! Should you even *think* of giving him or any other impoverished creature shelter, it will be the last thought you have as my employee! Do I make myself clear?"

The innkeeper's face was red, his eyes mere slits in his puffy cheeks.

"I understand. I'll make sure he leaves immediately."

"And that beggar boy—" Ebenezer gestured to the front room.

Aaron stood up straight. Ebenezer might be able to push him around, but he wasn't going to let anybody insult his family. Job or no job, it wasn't going to happen.

"He's not a beggar. He's my son!"

The innkeeper was only momentarily taken aback.

"Get him out of here! He's bad for business. People will think we're giving handouts! Or"—Ebenezer sneered— "is that what you had in mind? Make a little extra money by having your son here? Make people feel sorry for him? Maybe give him a shekel or two? Hmm?"

Aaron let loose his grip on anger. "I have never given you any reason to doubt my intentions or question my work. My family came to bring me a meal. That's all."

"Well, I don't want that boy here. Besides, you don't have time to socialize. When you're here, you work! You visit with your family on your own time." Ebenezer shoved Aaron against the wall as he turned to go back to his private room, shouting over his shoulder, "As far as that man is concerned, his family can go bed down with the sheep, for all I care!"

Aaron took deep breaths and tried to gather himself. In his desire to help, Timothy had just made a bad situation worse. In his compassion, he'd led Joseph to believe he'd have a place to stay. Now Aaron was going to have to tell Joseph he couldn't help him. And his wife was pregnant.

Aaron dreaded what he was being forced to do. Timothy had never seen him in this position—had never known Aaron *not* to help someone—but Aaron couldn't afford to lose his job. It was that simple. Between his small salary and the cost of Timothy's medications, he was barely able to put food on the table.

Returning to the front room, Aaron could feel the stares. Even over the commotion, people had heard Ebenezer's tirade. His face felt hot with embarrassment.

"Father, you're still going to help Mary and Joseph find a place to stay, right? I mean, you can't just leave them with no place to go."

"I'm sorry Timothy. There's nothing I can do."

The expression on his son's face changed from concern to disbelief. "But, Father, if you don't help them, who will?"

"Timothy, don't worry," said Joseph. "Mary and I will be fine. We'll find a place to stay."

"But it's going to be dark soon!"

"Son, you know I'd help if I could, but I can't."

Joseph said, "Please don't be angry, Timothy. It's not your father's fault. Now, come on. Walk with me. Let's go find Mary and your mother."

Timothy's entire body slumped in deep dejection.

"Thank you again for protecting my son," said Aaron to Joseph. Then he knelt before Timothy. "And I'm sorry if I let you down."

The boy didn't say a word. He didn't even look back to say good-bye.

Aaron's heart felt heavier than it had in a long, long time. Helpless and hopeless. He saw no way to change either.

★　★　★

He could feel her piercing stare before he saw her. Martha was standing there.

"What's wrong? Why isn't Timothy with you?"

Martha marched to face her husband. "Because he's across the street with the couple you just turned away!"

She wouldn't make a scene or disrespect him, but he could tell she wanted a first-hand account of what happened. What he'd done to Mary and Joseph was so out of character, she had worried.

"Ebenezer's greed is out of control. He's consumed with how much he can profit by the registration." Aaron took Martha by the elbow, and maneuvered her back toward the doorway. "Please. Take Timothy home and stay there. I don't want Ebenezer to see you anywhere close to the inn. If you want me to keep my job, please do as I ask." Aaron's voice was firm.

She nodded. By her expression, Aaron knew Martha understood the gravity of the situation. "Come home as soon as you can."

Aaron watched as she made her way across the street.

Day had given way to night. The strange star was directly overhead. The darker the sky, the brighter its light. They had noticed the star months ago. Over time, it moved closer and closer to Bethlehem. Now, the celestial body seemed to stall. That was fine with Aaron. It was beautiful.

"Excuse me! Might you be the man I should talk to about a room?"

Aaron was so caught up in looking at the star that he hadn't realized the gentleman was speaking to him.

"Oh, I apologize. I didn't mean to ignore you. I was just admiring the star."

"Understandable." The man looked up. "Spectacular, isn't it?

Both men gazed at the sky.

Aaron broke away first. The last thing he wanted was for

Ebenezer to see him focused on anything but work. "Now, you were asking about accommodations?"

The two men walked toward the big table where guests were to sign their names.

"I hope you still have something available," said the man. "As much as I enjoy the starlight, I'm ready to sleep with a roof over my head."

"We have one room left." Aaron hated doing it, but he quoted him the price. It was wrong to charge this much for a place to sleep.

The man didn't seem the slightest bit surprised or concerned. He signed the registry and paid the fee.

Well, Ebenezer got his wish. There's officially no more room at the inn.

Six

Ebenezer picked up his ledgers from the table.

He couldn't wait to get home. He wanted some peace and quiet and to breathe without feeling woozy. His headache had returned. He couldn't get out of the inn quickly enough, which was unusual. He'd spent many nights here, counting, adding, subtracting. Oh, how he loved numbers.

Ebenezer bullied his way through the room, seeking fresh air, but there were so many people between him and the door, it was slow going. He'd barked his final instructions to Aaron, who simply nodded in acknowledgment. He had to admit, he'd never seen his assistant so assertive as he was today. It had taken him by surprise.

He'll never speak to me like that again, I guarantee!

Ebenezer was almost at the entrance. He paused. He wanted to be able to hurry through the doorway so he wasn't stalled next to the mezuzah. Though he knew he'd not really seen a face, it unnerved him, and he didn't want anything to dampen his mood. The inn was full!

People parted, and he took advantage of it, but just as he started to plow through, a soldier stepped in front of the opening. Ebenezer had to pause until the soldier passed.

He tried to avert his eyes, but he saw it in his peripheral vision. A face. Still that of a woman, but not the same as earlier. He was so startled he bolted, ramming into the Roman.

The soldier shoved Ebenezer, and told him to watch where he was going.

The innkeeper tripped, and dropped one of the heavy ledgers. He was instantly infuriated. The book was precious to him. Nobody, not even this boy soldier, was going to disrespect his hard work.

When Ebenezer tried to pick it up, the guard put the point of his spear on the black leather cover. Without thinking, Ebenezer knocked the spear away. He jumped to his feet, and stood face-to-face with the man. The innkeeper glared, and the guard took a step back.

"You may think you can treat me like these other peasants"—Ebenezer gestured around him—"but you have no idea who you're dealing with. I can have you whipped until you beg for mercy. And don't think I won't. Now out of my way!"

The Roman guard looked uncertain what to do. He backed away from Ebenezer, but with a warning to watch his attitude or he'd be the one under the whip.

Ebenezer just grunted, cursing under his breath. As he adjusted his robe and dusted off the ledger, he glanced back at the door frame. Nothing unusual.

He moved on.

★　✱　✱

Once Ebenezer passed through the main square, his pace quickened. He kept glancing over his shoulder. Though he didn't see anyone, he felt a presence, as if someone followed him. He thought he could even feel breath on his neck.

Then he heard his name. It was almost a whisper, as if spoken a long way off and carried on the wind.

Impossible. Just like the apparitions in the doorway. Probably too much wine, consumed too quickly. He chose not to acknowledge the morning encounter, for he'd consumed no wine prior to it.

He saw his home ahead. The sooner he got there, the better.

The ledgers felt heavier than usual. In the past, he had no problem bringing them home. This time, however, he struggled to open the gate and dropped one of the books. The twine binding loosened, and pages scattered. He had to put the other books down to retrieve the pages before the breeze carried them away.

By the time he made it back to the gate, he was out of breath and sweating heavily. He leaned against the gate.

That's when he saw it. A man's face in the crumbling mezuzah. Crying out, he fell backward, landing hard on his bottom.

Crawling, he grabbed the ledgers from the ground and practically rolled into the courtyard. Ebenezer had never moved so fast. He stumbled to the door, and somehow managed to open it. Once inside, he slammed it with such force, the noise reverberated around the room. He stood rigid, staring at the back of the door, waiting.

Nothing.

Ebenezer scanned the room. There was a large, heavy table in the entry hall. Dropping the ledgers to the floor, he strove to push the table to block the front door. Fear coursed through his body, lending him strength. Finally, he managed to maneuver the table close enough that the door couldn't easily swing open.

His heart hammered in his chest. He thought he might pass out, but he stood still, listening. The only sound was the whistling wheeze of his breath.

Finally, his heart slowed, and he backed away. He tripped over the ledgers he'd thrown down in his panic. Ebenezer retrieved them and went into the parlor, setting them on the low table. Completely spent, he dropped to the floor cushions, his mind scrambling.

What was happening to him? Was this exhaustion? He'd been working every day from sunup to sundown, but that was nothing new. Was he ill?

His stomach growled, and he realized he'd not eaten since early morning. *That explains it! I'm weak from hunger, and had too much wine on an empty stomach.* It still didn't explain the morning incident, but maybe he hadn't eaten enough the night before.

He looked at the hearth. Cold as death. He'd build a fire, heat something to eat, enjoy a cup of wine, and read his ledgers. That's precisely what he needed. A peaceful night with no distractions.

Ebenezer talked himself into feeling calm. He was still a little apprehensive, but no longer afraid.

He built a small fire and lit a few lamps. Ebenezer spent most of his time either in Jerusalem or at the inn, so he thought it absurd to spend money on candles, wood, or oil. Even though it strained his eyes to see in low light, he preferred it. Light was expensive. Darkness was free.

He found the pot of gruel he'd had the night before. It resembled something one would use in construction, but with a good wine to wash it down, it would suffice.

While the lumpy, grey concoction heated, he carried a lamp into his room. He removed his outer robe. It reeked of dried wine, sweat, and the saturated stench from the inn. He threw the garment on the floor and kicked it to the corner. The woman who washed his clothes could pick it up.

He had no other household help. As far as he was concerned, what he couldn't see past the sphere of his lamp didn't exist. Why pay someone to clean it?

When he was stripped down to his undergarment, Ebenezer went to the basin to wash. The water pitcher was empty. He thought of filling it, then decided to forgo the bath. Though there was surely a perfectly good explanation for the strange occurrences of the day, it didn't mean he wanted to go back outside. He wiped his hands on a towel. That was good enough.

Ebenezer returned to the front room, poured a goblet of wine, and sat down. He told himself to drink slowly. Savor the taste, allow it to help calm his mind. He took several deep breaths and closed his eyes. He habitually rubbed the stem of his goblet between his fingers. Yes. This was just what he needed.

He leaned back, and rested the goblet on his chest. The cup was encircled by precious stones which had been carved and faceted into the shape of diamonds. Instead of the usual long and slender stem, this one was thick, its edges squared. The Roman Seal was stamped on one side. The base was wide, with intricate carvings of animals around the bottom. Yes, this goblet was meant for only those with power and wealth. That's why he kept the other chalice at work. It was a symbol. He was in control.

Aaron never asked where the goblet came from. Surely he wondered. But then again, maybe not. Ebenezer never took the time to carry on any type of sociable conversation with the man. He really didn't know anything about Aaron except that he had a family and was a God-fearing, law-abiding man. Aaron refused to work on the Sabbath, so Ebenezer made sure he worked longer hours the rest of the week. The "day of rest" was a lazy man's way of picking the innkeeper's pocket every seven days.

Ebenezer thought about his assistant. Until today, he had no idea that Aaron had a crippled child. Not that it mattered. Wasn't any of his business. Didn't affect Ebenezer one way or the other. All he cared about was that the man did his job. Still, today he'd seen a side of Aaron that had never manifested itself before. He wasn't quite sure how he felt about it.

"Oh, well. I have better things to do than think about Aaron or his crippled son."

Ebenezer dished out some of the gruel. It plopped in his bowl in a sticky, gooey mound. It looked disgusting. He shrugged. He was eating for function. His wine was for enjoying.

He sat back down and ate a few mouthfuls of the mush, then washed it down with the wine. It made it palatable. Barely. Ebenezer stared into the fire. After a few more bites, he set the bowl aside. Enough of that.

Laying back, he once again rested his cup on his chest. He loved the way the gems sparkled in the firelight. His eyes grew heavy. The specters, the repugnant odors, the conflicts—time to put them all behind him. It wasn't long before Ebenezer fell asleep.

Seven

When Ebenezer finally walked out of the inn with his precious ledgers, the relief was so great, Aaron felt several pounds lighter. A heavy burden was lifted off his shoulders. He still had troubles, but at least for now, he was free of Ebenezer. He knew the man might come back. He'd done it before. Like a surprise test, Ebenezer hoped to catch him off guard, slacking on the job. But, for the moment, Aaron could breathe.

He went into a small alcove off the front room. It was blocked by a thick, wooden door. Checking to make sure no one followed him, Aaron entered then secured the door behind him. Stacked on a table were several metal boxes, each with a lock that could only be opened with a specific key. Usually Ebenezer held on to the keys so no one could gain access without going to him first, but before he left, the innkeeper had entrusted Aaron with them—accompanied by a warning that, should the money in the boxes not equal the amounts due, Aaron would not only lose his job, but stand trial for thievery. Then Ebenezer assured him he would be found guilty and stoned.

As he unlocked the box, Aaron shook his head. It must be terrible to live like Ebenezer. Never happy, always judging, always fearing someone was out to swindle him. To never trust another human being must be the loneliest feeling in the world.

Aaron counted the money for the third time to make sure the accounts added up, then locked the money away.

Returning to the front room, he stopped short. There was Caleb, his oldest son, straining his neck to search the room.

"Caleb!"

The boy jumped.

"I don't know what's going on, but your mother seems determined to disobey me. I told her to make sure all of you went home. I—"

"Father, we know what you told Mother, but she said I must come and find you." The boy was clearly in distress.

"What's wrong?"

"Mother said you need to come to the well."

"She knows I can't leave."

"Mary, the wife of the man who helped Timothy—"

"What about her?"

"She's hurt, and they need a place to stay."

"And just what am I supposed to do about it? There's no room here, and I have no idea where there is!" Aaron was growing more impatient and frustrated with his wife. She had never before been a cause for discontent, but today, of all days, she seemed intent on doing just that.

Caleb just shrugged, and shook his head.

Aaron heaved a sigh, and ran his fingers through his beard. "You say the woman is hurt. Did she fall?"

Caleb didn't know. Just that his mother said to hurry and fetch his father.

As exasperated as Aaron was, he knew Martha wouldn't have sent their son to get him if it wasn't vital. He looked around the room. Things seemed to be under control. Ebenezer's room was secured, and the money was locked away. Nobody appeared to need his attention. Maybe he could leave for a few minutes. But no more.

"Tell your mother I'm on my way."

Caleb started to leave, then turned back. "Father? I almost forgot. Mother said to bring some cloth and the salve you use when you cut your hands. She said you'd know what she was talking about. Oh, and I need to bring jars for water."

Aaron nodded. "You know where the jars are. I'll collect the other things and be there shortly."

He found the healing cream and the cloth—wide pieces for cleaning, narrower strips for bandaging. He made one last sweep of the inn, making sure everyone had what they needed, then walked out the door.

Would this day never end?

★　★　★

He found the small group sitting on the wall adjacent to the well. Joseph introduced Aaron to Mary.

Martha asked if he would walk with her a moment. Aaron was more than willing. He wanted an explanation, and to find out what she proposed he do. It didn't matter, really. He wouldn't do it because he couldn't do it. He had to get back to the inn.

"I believe Mary's in the early stages of labor," Martha said in a matter-of-fact voice. "And her feet need attention."

"Her feet?"

Martha looked up at Aaron and simply said, "You'll see. Then you can make up your mind on whether to help this couple or let them be."

Aaron studied her face. This wasn't going to be that simple. "Martha—"

She'd already turned to walk back.

He looked at the sky. The star was definitely brighter. Bigger, it seemed.

Simple? Shaking his head, Aaron muttered. "Nothing is simple anymore. Nothing."

★   ★   ★

When he rejoined the group, both Joseph and Martha were kneeling in front of Mary. Timothy was on the wall, sitting next to her. It was the first time Aaron really saw the woman's face. He was surprised to see how young she was, not much older than his eldest daughter.

Martha leaned back so Aaron could observe Mary's feet. Normally, such a thing would never be done. Exposing a woman's ankles was frowned upon. For a man to look at another man's wife in such a way was unheard of. He quickly turned away.

"Aaron." It was Joseph. "It's all right."

Aaron knelt next to him, and saw how difficult and painful this was going to be. Difficult for Joseph. Painful for Mary. There was no getting around it. Mary's sandals had to be cut off her feet. He had no idea how she was even walking. Cracked, caked with dried blood and dirt, the woman's feet were so swollen, the leather straps made deep dents in the skin. Martha washed Mary's feet, revealing a worse situation: the leather was embedded into the tight, tumid folds of skin.

Joseph was shaking. Not only was he nervous, he was beside himself with guilt. He kept telling Mary over and over how sorry he was for not realizing her predicament. Even with her reassurances, it was obvious the man felt like a failure as a husband.

So, cutting the straps was Aaron's job. Joseph said he had the steadier hands.

If he only knew.

Slowly, carefully, Aaron managed to cut through one strap at a time. In several instances, it required he cut Mary's skin to release the leather. Blood pooled on the ground. Mary never complained, and sat perfectly still. He glanced at her face, and a single tear trickled down her cheek. Martha kept her arm around Mary and pulled her close, whispering in soft motherly tones. Timothy held her hand.

Aaron had a huge lump in his throat. He wanted to stop the couple's suffering—the woman's physical pain, and the man's mental turmoil. He was ashamed he'd considered otherwise.

Finally, the sandals were cut free. Martha tended to Mary's wounds. Her feet were bleeding profusely. Aaron wondered if he'd need to return to the inn for more cloth. Joseph smoothed his wife's hair and looked anxious.

Martha glanced at Aaron and gave a quick nod, a signal that he should remove Joseph from the scene. Aaron took Joseph by the arm, and they walked away. Neither man spoke. Aaron couldn't find the right words.

"Excuse me." A man holding the reins of a beautiful mare was walking in their direction. "Can either of you men tell me where I'd go to talk to someone about keeping my horse in that corral?" He pointed to the roped area next to the inn.

Aaron glanced at Joseph. "I'll be right back."

He helped the man with his horse, then ducked back inside the inn to make the financial arrangements. He was relieved to see things were still peaceful. Patrons had settled down. Conversations were calmer, tempers subdued. Many had fallen asleep. Despite that, he couldn't stay away for long.

When Aaron went outside, he saw that Joseph had returned to the group at the well. Joining them, he could see something else was going on. "What's happened.?"

Martha wiped the back of her wrist across her damp forehead. "Mary's in labor."

Concern filled Joseph's eyes. "She can't stay here."

A horse in the corral whinnied and bumped the rail with its nose. She obviously didn't care for the accommodations. Aaron shook his head at the ungrateful beast. *Stop complaining. At least you have a place to stay.*

Wait. Maybe—

"I have an idea."

Joseph jumped off the wall. "What is it?"

"Don't get too excited. It's not good, but it's something that might work temporarily."

"It doesn't matter."

"That corral. Ebenezer had me build it when he first heard about the registration. It was a way for him to make more money. For a *small* fee, guests could keep their animals close by. That way, they could keep an eye on them and easily leave immediately after registering. Our real stable is down the hill, behind the inn."

The idea sounded better in his head. Saying it out loud made it sound ridiculous.

"Go on."

Aaron took a deep breath and continued. "I was the last one at the stable. I cleaned out all the old hay, animal waste, cobwebs, everything. I covered the floor with fresh hay, and there are several jars we can fill with clean water. It's private, and it's quiet. Nobody will know you're even there."

Joseph said nothing.

Aaron felt more uncomfortable by the moment. He'd just suggested this man and his wife, who was about to deliver a baby, should stay in a cave meant to house animals. "I'm sorry. It was a foolish idea, and—"

Joseph cut him off. "The perfect solution."

"No, it's far from perfect. Your baby will be born in a stable! This is not a solution."

Smiling, Joseph gripped Aaron's shoulder. "Yes, it is."

"What?" Martha balled her hands into fists, and put them on her hips. Not a good sign. Martha only stood like that when one of the children was in trouble. "Putting a pregnant woman in a stable? That's the most absurd idea I've ever heard! Fresh hay, clean water! So what? It's still a cave!"

Aaron agreed, but he had nothing better.

"Well, there has to be something else. We're not going to—"

"I think it's a wonderful idea." It was the first time Aaron had heard the woman speak. Mary was sipping water and sitting up straight. She had a little more color in her cheeks.

Martha wasn't so easily convinced. "There just has to be somewhere else."

Nobody said anything. There were no other ideas forthcoming.

Martha sighed and took charge. "Caleb, you lead the donkey. Make sure those bundles are secure. I'll try to find sandals for Mary. Meantime, Joseph, you're going to have to lift her to the donkey. I'll meet you shortly. I must go home first and gather supplies. Aaron—"

Aaron felt so conflicted that he didn't even know in what direction to look. Toward the inn? The only financial security his family had? Or did he stay with the young couple who was being forced to spend an undetermined amount of time living in a stable? To have their first child born in a cave? If ever he needed God to show him what to do, it was now.

"Father?"

Everyone turned to look at Timothy. He'd not said a word until now.

Aaron stood in front of his son. "What is it?"

"Don't worry, Father. Everything is going to be all right."

"What makes you say that?"

Timothy put his arms out so Aaron would pick him up. "I just know. That's all."

Aaron held him close.

Timothy whispered in Aaron's ear, "God told me."

Aaron looked at the boy. "He did?"

Timothy nodded.

Most people would have laughed at such a notion—the Almighty speaking to a child—but Aaron knew Timothy. The boy wouldn't have said it if he didn't truly believe it.

Aaron picked up the boy's crutch. "Well, then, let's you and me show them the way."

As they began to make their way toward the stable, Aaron glanced over his shoulder toward the inn.

If this was truly God's idea, then he hoped God also had plans to rescue him if Ebenezer ever found out.

Eight

*E*benezer cried out against excruciating pain. Blood dripped down his side as the soldier pierced his ribcage with his sword. He jerked, and tried to move away. More blood. Sticky. Warm.

He snorted awake, his gaze darted around the room.

His room. He was at home.

He sat up. His garments were wet, but not from blood. It was red wine. The pain in his side came from rolling over on the gold chalice. What a dream! He'd been crucified. The soldier thrusting the sword into his side was the guard he ran into when leaving the inn.

Ebenezer grunted and cursed. He stood, and his wine-soaked gown stuck to his skin.

He went to his room and removed his wet, stained tunic. He kicked it into the corner with the other dirty robe. Ebenezer remembered he had no water, so he wiped off what he could and put on a clean tunic.

Ebenezer thought of going on to bed, but realized he was no longer sleepy. He had no idea how long he'd slept.

He stoked the small fire, and lit another lamp. He filled his goblet, retrieved a ledger, and began studying the numbers. He

wanted to see what his profit might be after the registration was over. He was almost giddy with anticipation.

He had supplied many of the animals used for sacrifices at the temple during Passover. Over three hundred thousand Jews had poured into Jerusalem. Most had to buy their lambs and doves after they arrived. The cost for the convenience was well beyond what most could pay, but they had no recourse, and Ebenezer took financial advantage of their situation. The figures were up from the previous year.

Ebenezer looked at the next column of numbers. He had made some very lucrative loans to those who owed taxes. He overcharged, and demanded immediate payments. The monetary penalty was exorbitant, and he had no problem in turning those who were delinquent over to the authorities. Ebenezer paid only a fraction of the taxes required of others, thus allowing him to make an even greater profit from each transaction. The total was more than he'd anticipated.

And now the Jews had to register so Rome could levy even more taxes. Oh, it was going to be a very good year. Ebenezer was almost salivating.

He sat back and thought about his money. He had more than he would ever spend in his lifetime, and should he die anytime soon, he had no idea what would happen to it. There was no charitable organization he believed in. He certainly wasn't going to leave it to his nephew.

He bristled. Isaac would never see a shekel of his money. Never!

But Ebenezer didn't need worry about such things. He wasn't going to die any time soon. He still had years to increase his bank account. Who knew how wealthy he'd be when his time came? He may just have his money buried with him. That way, he'd be sure no ungrateful, lazy pauper would get one coin of it.

Ebenezer gazed at the fire.

At one time, the hearth had been an artistic masterpiece. The marble tiles were hand-painted scenes depicting Jewish history. One in particular illustrated the pillar of fire when God led the Jews out of Egypt. The fire in the painting began to spin. The faster it turned, the bigger it grew until it burst from the tile.

Clutching the goblet, Ebenezer rushed behind a chair, and stared at the flames in terror.

The flames twirled, and grew to almost twice his height. He heard his name, sizzling through the heat like steam.

A spark separated from the column and flashed around the room like a shooting star across the sky. It bounced from wall to wall, and flew over his head. The flame grew hotter, the voice calling his name grew louder, and the spark hung only inches from his face. He screamed, threw his precious goblet in the air, and dove under the floor cushions, pulling them over his head. The thundering pandemonium would surely burst his ear drums, and the scalding heat burn him alive.

Suddenly, the room went quiet. Ebenezer waited, then slowly raised his head and stood. Everything was still. Then, from behind him, he heard his name.

"Ebenezer!"

Standing in a pillar of fire was a man.

It called his name again, and reached out to Ebenezer as if to pull him into an embrace.

Ebenezer shook uncontrollably.

The light became brighter and brighter, blinding him. He covered his eyes.

Then, all grew quiet. Ebenezer slowly uncovered his eyes. The figure still stood before him, and the innkeeper fell to his knees.

"Who are you?"

"I am the angel Gabriel. I have a message for you."

"What message? From whom?"

"God."

Ebenezer dropped his hands and laughed. "An angel! From God? Ha! You're nothing but a figment of my imagination! You're no more an angel than this pillow!"

Ebenezer threw the cushion at the man. It passed right through.

The light burst into flames again. The figure was still inside. Its voice thundered, reverberating around the room.

Ebenezer covered his ears, yet even with his eyes closed, he was blinded. He had to escape.

He remembered the basin across the room, but it was empty. The door was blocked by the table. He was trapped in a prison of his own making.

"What do you want from me?"

"Much!" The voice boomed.

He screamed and crawled around the room, searching for cover. He hurled at the light anything within reach. Cushions, pottery, even a precious ledger. Everything went sailing through the apparition as if nothing were there.

The light became a spark once again and flew to hang in front of Ebenezer's face.

He pleaded with the light to cease its torment. "Who are you? What are you? Why do you torture me this way?"

The light settled in the center of the room. Slowly a man appeared.

Ebenezer bowed down. Not out of respect, but because he didn't want to look at him. Common sense refused to acknowledge the apparition, yet he knew there was some sort of presence before him. "You say you are a messenger from God?"

"I am Gabriel."

"What do you want from me?" Ebenezer's voice cracked. His throat was parched.

"You don't believe me." It was not a question, but a statement of fact.

Ebenezer raised his head, and tried to sound confident. "I didn't earlier, and I don't now."

"If I'm not real, why do you continue trying to convince yourself I don't exist? What evidence do you require?"

Slowly, Ebenezer surveyed the room. Because of the angel's light, he could see every corner. He stopped short at a cobweb-covered shelf. He squinted to see the small silver bell, barely visible through the filth. He'd forgotten it was there.

"Do you see that bell?"

"I do."

Ebenezer scoffed. "You're not even looking at it."

"Nevertheless, I see it. The bell belonged to your sister. It was tied around the neck of her favorite lamb. When she died, you had the lamb slaughtered."

Ebenezer froze. No one knew where the bell came from. No one! He slowly turned to face the angel. The light brightened. Tears mixed with sweat stung his eyes. Hiding his face he exclaimed, "You're blinding me!"

Gabriel's voice roared, "You were already blind!"

The light dimmed.

Ebenezer snuffled and wiped his nose with his sleeve. "Why are you here?"

"I've been sent here for your redemption."

"From what do I need to be redeemed?"

"Your life. Your greedy, insignificant, useless life. You have never looked beyond the money you count to see from where it comes. You ignore the cries of the hungry, the poor, and the sick. Your heart is cold, and you waste your days in a world of parchment and coins."

"But I am a good businessman!"

"Your business does no good."

"How is it you know what I do?"

"I have sat by you, traveled with you, and listened to your useless prattle many a day."

"Then why do you show yourself to me now?"

Gabriel moved closer to Ebenezer, who screamed for mercy.

"I hear your cries for mercy. You plead for it, but I have none to give. You ask for comfort, but have no heart to receive it. Instead, I offer you a chance for redemption. You have done your part to fulfill the prophecies of old. Now you must choose how you will react to those things that have come to pass, and the things yet to be. It will be your choice, Ebenezer, and yours alone. There is life after death, and this night you will choose how and where you will spend it."

Ebenezer's voice was hoarse. "What prophecy? How do I make a choice if I don't know what you're talking about?"

"The baby whose coming was foretold will be born this very night in the city of David. The King will be born, not in a palace, but in a stable with a throne made of wood and hay. You have seen to it that this prophecy is fulfilled."

Ebenezer cursed. It slipped out before he could stop it. He ducked, sure that Gabriel would swoop down and burn him, but the angel remained where he was.

"Your response is all I expected it to be. My time grows short, so listen well. Three more of my kind will come to you. Without them, you have no chance at finding your redemption. Expect the first when you hear the bell ring."

Ebenezer squirmed. "Couldn't they just all come at once?"

"The second will appear with the next ring," Gabriel continued as if the man had not spoken. The angel rose and diminished in size, becoming lost in the light once more.

"But you mentioned *three* visitors!" Ebenezer realized he didn't want the angel to leave. He wanted to hear more about what to expect.

The light was the size of a small plate. Gabriel's voice was faint but clear. "The third angel appears when it is his time. Look for me no more. Remember all I have spoken. For your own sake, Ebenezer, do not forget."

The light shrank to the size of a coin, then disappeared completely.

★   ✳   ✳

Ebenezer looked around the room. Without the light of the angel, it seemed especially dark and dirty. The fire in the hearth had died down to embers. The only evidence of his unwelcome guest was the strewn cushions and shattered pottery.

He spotted his sister's bell. It had been years since he'd touched it. Carefully making his way through the darkened room, he picked it up, wiped away the dust, and saw that it had intricate designs etched in the metal. It was beautiful. Just like his sister.

"Dear sister. You were everything the angel says I am not. I can't argue with that. As for the rest of it—" He placed the bell on the table in front of the hearth.

Ebenezer decided to move the large barrier blocking the front door. He figured the angels would come regardless. As he began to push the table, the room became brighter. Light came through a small window and through the crack under the door. The beam was a soft whitish blue.

"Could it be my first visitor is here already? Gabriel said I'd hear a bell. I've heard no ring."

Finally there was enough space for Ebenezer to slip out the door. He edged his way into the courtyard. It was filled with light.

"I've never seen such a magnificent sight. Why, I could read by the light of that star!"

Ebenezer looked around and saw a bench next to the wall. He had no idea how or when it got there, but now he brushed it off and sat down. Leaning back, he stared at the heavenly brilliance and inhaled deeply.

He raised his nose. *What is that fragrance? It's so sweet and so*—Ebenezer breathed in and out—*familiar.* He inhaled once more. *I can't place it.*

He looked around the courtyard. Weeds poked through cracks in the stone. At one time the courtyard was probably beautiful, but so long ago he couldn't remember how it must have appeared. He didn't dwell on it. The fountain was dry and full of debris. Stone figures were missing parts of their physical appearance. Yet, because of the incredible fragrance wafting around him, the courtyard didn't seem so ugly.

He let the soft breeze caress his face, and his eyes grew heavy. Under the starlit sky, Ebenezer fell asleep.

★ ★ ★

Ebenezer woke, startled and sore. He had a stiff neck, and his lower back ached from sleeping upright on the stone bench while leaning against the rock wall. Stretching, he tried to remember why he was even in the courtyard. His confusion was brief as he looked around the starlit enclosure. The gentle breeze swept his hair across his brow. The lovely fragrance still permeated the air.

Ebenezer tried to piece together the events of the previous evening. He had no idea how long he'd been asleep. Then he remembered the angel's visit. Maybe it had all been a bad dream, but—what was it Gabriel had said? When the bell rings, three more angels would come.

He cursed.

The thought of his sister's bell was enough to return Ebenezer to his normal crotchety, pessimistic self. Taking one last glance at the gorgeous sky, he stomped back inside. Enough of this nonsense! To believe all the occurrences from the day before were more than a bad dream was a pure waste of time.

Walking by the table in front of the hearth, he saw his sister's bell. It lay there as quiet as death. *Just like you, dear sister.*

If the bell was free from cobwebs and dirt, what would he find if he lit a lamp? Would he see more evidence of the pandemonium from earlier? He opted to make his way to his room by the shaft of light through the window.

Ebenezer wasn't sure how to identify his emotions. All he knew was that his heart was heavy and he didn't like it. All this sentimental rubbish wore on his nerves. The more he thought, the more perplexed he became. He decided it was nothing that a profitable day's work couldn't fix. And, in order to be at his best, he figured the best thing to do would be to try to salvage as much sleep as he could from what was left of this bizarre night.

★ ★ ★

Ebenezer would never know if it was mere moments or hours later when he was awakened by the sound of a child's laughter. It was followed by the soft tinkling of a bell. He quickly pulled his blanket up so only his eyes were exposed.

The covers were yanked back as if by some invisible hand. He covered his face with his hands.

"Ebenezer!"

The voice sounded like that of a child, and he splayed his fingers and peeked out. A strange figure stood at the foot of his bed. It *was* a child, though he couldn't tell if it was a male or female. It had long hair, almost white in color, and wore a pale blue tunic cinched at the waist by a glimmering gold belt. Draped in chains of flowers, and emanating an aroma Ebenezer had smelled earlier in the courtyard, the child was surrounded by a soft glow as if floating in perpetual sunlight. Between the angel's luminescence and the starlight filtering from the outer room, this might be morning.

The child began flitting around the room.

Finally finding his voice, Ebenezer asked, "Are you the angel Gabriel mentioned?"

"I am." The angel continued its aerobatics.

"What are you?"

"I am the angel of the past."

"Whose past?"

"Your past." The child angel flew close to the floor then swooped back up again.

"Stop moving in such a fashion. You're making me dizzy. And can you dim your light?"

The angel settled in front of the bed. "It's no wonder my light hurts your eyes. You've lived in the dark for so long, you're now more comfortable there. It allows you to remain blind to the hopelessness your darkness brings to all those you meet."

"Why have you come?"

The angel danced around the room once more, as if for the simple pleasure of it. "Your welfare."

"A good night's sleep would work just as well."

The angel settled weightlessly on Ebenezer's chest. "Come. Touch my heart." The child pointed to its chest.

"I know where the heart is," Ebenezer snapped.

"That surprises me, considering how long it's been since you've used yours."

The small angel grasped Ebenezer's hand, placing it over the being's heart, and immediately Ebenezer stood beside the angel without his feet ever touching the floor.

"I must dress."

"No need. No one can see us. These are only fragments of your past, Ebenezer. You've lived them. You cannot change them. It is too late for that."

"If I cannot alter them, then why must I see them?"

"It will remind you, Ebenezer, of what you had and what you lost, and what you chose to give up willingly."

The angel settled on the floor, still holding Ebenezer's hand. He could not tell if the angel was actually walking on two feet, or merely floating beside him. It didn't matter. He was heading into the unknown. But then again—

Nine

Ebenezer still grasped the small angel's hand, but now the pair stood on an open road under a clear, blue sky. Grain swayed in the breeze. Bethlehem had vanished.

"Good heavens!" Ebenezer spun around. "I was born near here. I worked these fields as a boy!"

He stood on his toes and shaded his eyes with his hand, looking one way then the other. Memories came flooding back. Joys, hopes, and disappointments long forgotten. He was conscious of aromas, each one connected to a different recollection.

The angel floated in front of Ebenezer. "Is your lip trembling?"

The innkeeper bit his lip and muttered, "Lead on."

"You don't remember the way?"

"I most certainly do. I could walk this road blindfolded."

The angel settled to walk beside Ebenezer. "It strikes me as odd that you recollect it so well, yet have forgotten the joy you felt here."

The bizarre couple continued down the road in momentary silence. Ebenezer recognized every landmark they passed. They followed a small stream as a group of boys ran along the banks, laughing and slinging sticks and pebbles into the clear water. They were happy, carefree.

Ebenezer exclaimed, and began calling them by name.

The angel reminded him, "These are but visions from your past, Ebenezer. They aren't aware of our presence."

As he watched the boys, Ebenezer recognized himself as one of those having the most fun. It had been so long since he'd experienced such joy, he didn't remember the sound of his own laughter.

"Look there." The angel floated ahead.

Ebenezer suddenly stood in front of a small synagogue where a group of boys gathered their scrolls. From their discussions, they were going home to celebrate the Sabbath. As each bid a farewell, Ebenezer called out, "Peace be with thee."

The angel looked at him.

Embarrassed, Ebenezer muttered under his breath.

Shrugging, the angel pointed, and the two were inside the synagogue.

"The school is not quite empty. A solitary child is left there still."

Ebenezer didn't have to look. He blinked back tears and said he knew.

They entered a bleak, sparsely-furnished, poorly-lit room. In the middle was an old rickety table covered with scrolls, open and yellowing. Sitting on the worn bench in front of a small fire was a boy. Ebenezer sat down next to him, and this time he couldn't control his tears. He wept at the sight of the child he used to be.

The boy burst out in amazement over something he was reading.

The angel rose, and peeked over the child's shoulder. "It's amazing how much happiness can come from a simple story. Adventures with imaginary characters."

Ebenezer quickly stood and pushed the angel. "They are stories of our ancestors. Those characters were real, carrying me to faraway lands of pharaohs, giants, and great armies. They took me to places where I didn't have to shiver in this foul place!" He looked back at the boy on the bench. "Poor child."

"What did you say?"

"Nothing. I said nothing." Then Ebenezer added, "I saw a boy today. He would, I'm certain, have delighted in these stories."

All the angel said was, "Let's see another day."

When Ebenezer glanced at where the angel pointed, he saw an older self at the same table, the room even more inhospitable. A young girl came rushing in, throwing her arms around his neck.

"Dear brother! It is so wonderful to see you! I never thought this day would come!" She danced around the other Ebenezer. Joy radiated from her.

"Your sister was small. A delicate woman." The angel settled beside Ebenezer.

"Yes. And loving." His gaze never left his sister.

The angel rose, and put itself between Ebenezer and the scene. "She died a young woman. I believe she left behind a child. A son."

"She did." Ebenezer tried to look around the angel, wanting to see his beloved sister once more.

"He lives but a short walk from your inn, yet you choose not to see him."

"I'm busy. Now take me away from here." Ebenezer maneuvered around the angel, turning in all directions, having no idea how to get away.

"So busy that you cannot spend even a Sabbath meal with him?"

"As I said, I don't have time. Running one's own business

requires diligence and attention to detail. I don't have time to squander on such frivolous activities."

"Your sister wouldn't consider such time frivolous."

Ebenezer tried to push the angel away, finding only air instead. "We'll never know, will we?"

"Just because you refuse to acknowledge the truth doesn't negate its existence."

Ebenezer sneered.

The angel floated in front of him and held out its hand. Ebenezer had no choice but to take it. Placing it on his heart, the angel said, "It's time to move on."

In only a moment, the scene changed.

"Do you know this place?"

"Know it?" Ebenezer smiled. "I was an apprentice here!"

Immediately the pair stood inside.

His former employer rose from the table and, rubbing his hands together, instructed a young Ebenezer, "No more work tonight! The sun is about to set, and we must clear away everything. We don't want to be late for Sabbath dinner!"

Ebenezer watched the scene play out. The candles, the prayers, the traditions. He remembered how cared for, how nurtured he felt under his mentor, Nehemiah. The kindly man had renewed his love for family and his faith in God. Seeing it all now awoke feelings and emotions he'd not felt in a very long time.

The angel floated beside Ebenezer's shoulder. "It's been years since you observed the Sabbath as a day to keep holy."

"A silly, sentimental waste of time."

"Nehemiah didn't think it silly. He did nothing but spend a few extra coins so you could share in their Sabbath."

"It had nothing to do with money. It was done to show his devotion to God. By allowing me to share in it, he gave me a family once again. It erased some of the burdens of my heart. He was a wealthy, powerful man, but his real wealth was his family and friends. His strengths were his kind words, his fairness and acts of charity toward all. Even the most insignificant deeds by others were rewarded and praised. For him, life was a gift, and the joy he derived from it was greater than any fortune."

The angel stared at Ebenezer. "You respected Nehemiah a great deal."

"Of course. Everyone did."

"Yet you couldn't be more different from the man you just described."

Before Ebenezer could respond, the scene change. He saw himself in the prime of his life, yet already his face appeared slightly drawn, and wrinkles had formed the beginning of his distinctive scowl. Sitting alone on a stone wall was a woman with tears on her face. It was an occasion Ebenezer clearly remembered, and knew the tears were his own doing. He informed the angel he had no need to see this day. He knew the conversation by heart.

The angel gave him no reprieve. Ebenezer was forced to hear the words once more.

"I have been replaced by an idol."

The younger Ebenezer began to pace. "What are you talking about? What idol has replaced you?"

"A golden one. The god of wealth. All of your hopes and dreams now revolve around profit. The pursuit of money consumes you, leaving little time for anything else. Especially those matters of the heart."

"There's nothing wrong with hard work and wanting to better oneself. It doesn't change how I feel about you. I do it *for* you. I want to be able to give you everything you deserve. Anything your heart desires."

"My heart desires you find the joy you once felt in our plans for the future. You wanted a business like Nehemiah's, the sound of happy children at your feet, and the laughter of friends around our table. These will never be enough. Now, the only sound that makes you happy is the clinking of coins. I cannot compete with that, Ebenezer, and I no longer want to try."

Spinning away from the angel, Ebenezer cried, "No! I won't watch anymore!" Tears stung his eyes. Pain and anger consumed him.

The unrelenting angel floated up behind the weeping innkeeper and, with unseen strength, forced him to face his past.

The woman stood. "Our contract is an old one, made years ago when we were both young and poor. Our families are long since gone. There is no longer a reason for it to be binding. So I release you, Ebenezer. I love you too much to commit you to a future where you would be unhappy."

The young Ebenezer tried to comfort the woman, but she moved out of his reach.

"My decision may hurt you. In reality, it is only bruising your pride. The pain won't last long, for soon it will be replaced with a sense of relief. You will be free to put all your time and energy into increasing your profits. I hope you will be happy in the life you have chosen, Ebenezer. May your gold keep you warm at night, and the coins rattling in your purse sound as glorious as a family's laughter."

With that, the woman turned and walked away.

Ebenezer stared at his dejected self sitting on the wall alone. "Angel, show me no more. I don't need to see the things that no longer matter. Take me home!"

"This is your past, Ebenezer. You made your choices."

Enraged, he turned on the angel, grabbing and shaking it. He screamed at the floating child. The angel smiled at Ebenezer and gave him no resistance. Instead, its light grew brighter and brighter.

In his anger, Ebenezer was not aware at first that he had

returned to his own room and was wringing his blanket with both hands. He released it, and before he had another thought, he collapsed on the bed and sank into a heavy sleep.

Ten

Timothy couldn't help being slow, but Aaron grew increasingly impatient.

The entire day had required him to be calm. Because of the registration, he'd worked harder than he ever had before. Ebenezer had been merciless in his preparations, determined to maximize every opportunity for profit, and that meant taking full advantage of his employee. Ebenezer's verbal abuse had escalated, as evidenced by his outbursts during the day. Maybe the man was becoming unbalanced.

The guests had been demanding and short-tempered, and dealing with them had drained Aaron. And now this. It wasn't that he didn't want to help Mary and Joseph—they couldn't help their situation. However, it affected his job. His family's future. He would make sure the couple had what they needed, but he couldn't risk being away from the inn for long.

He picked up Timothy and placed him on his shoulders. They had to move more quickly. Following behind them, Caleb led the donkey while Mary rode. She was in pain from the terrible condition of her feet, and though the contractions were still far apart, there was no doubt she was in labor. Joseph walked beside her to make sure she didn't fall off the small donkey's back. Martha had left the group to gather supplies from home.

"Father?"

"Yes, son?" Aaron had to be careful. The path was rocky, with crevices and gullies hidden beneath the loose stones. The last thing he wanted was to drop Timothy.

"Something extraordinary is happening, isn't it?"

Aaron didn't respond. He still remembered Timothy saying that God told him everything would be all right. "I'm not sure what you mean."

"The star. It's different from any stars we've ever seen. 'The people who walk in darkness shall see a great light.' Father, do you think Isaiah was talking about the star?"

"Isaiah never mentioned the light coming from a star."

"Yes, but he spoke about a great light shining down on the people of Galilee and Judea, and about a child being born whose name would be called Wonderful Counselor, the Mighty God—"

Both finished the prophecy together, "'The everlasting Father, the Prince of Peace.'"

Timothy spent long hours studying the scriptures. His knowledge surpassed many who'd studied them their entire lives. The local rabbi was amazed at Timothy's knowledge, and enjoyed when he'd visit the synagogue to ask questions. But this was different. This was—Aaron wasn't comfortable even contemplating such a thing.

The child was relentless. "What about Micah?"

"The prophet Micah?"

"Yes. He said that Bethlehem would be the birthplace of a king."

Again, Aaron didn't respond right away. He slipped and caught himself in time to avoid falling. The closer they came to the bottom of the hill, the more rugged the terrain. They had to traverse all the dirt and stones that had, over time, rolled or been washed down the hill. The group was forced to slow down. Regardless of the star's importance, Aaron was glad for the light.

"Father?"

"What?" Aaron felt his patience dwindling again.

"What about Micah?" Timothy wiggled.

"Be still. You're going to make us fall."

The boy settled and was quiet.

"Timothy, I'm sorry. I didn't mean to sound like I don't care about your questions."

"You have a lot on your mind." Timothy kissed the top of his father's head.

"You asked me about Micah. What about him?"

"He said Bethlehem would be the birthplace of a king."

Aaron stopped and looked up at his son, speaking quietly so the others would not hear. "Timothy, maybe there *is* something amazing happening here in Bethlehem, but until we know for certain, let's keep this to ourselves. Especially don't mention it to Mary and Joseph. If you're wrong, they may think you and I have lost our minds."

"Does this mean you think I'm right?"

Aaron took a deep breath and let it out slowly. "I honestly don't know what I think." He glanced at the star. "I honestly don't know."

"Don't worry. I won't say anything. If the prophecies *are* coming true, I won't have to say anything." Timothy smiled down at his father. "The entire world will know."

Aaron's thoughts were far different. *Impossible. That's what it is. Impossible.*

The little group reached the bottom of the hill. Joseph carried Mary to the cave entrance while Caleb relieved the donkey of its parcels. The poor animal needed the rest.

"Father, I'll carry these skins and fill them with water," Caleb said. "Daniel is coming back with Mother, so he and I can fill the jars."

Aaron thanked his son then went into the stable and found the lamps he'd left in the entrance. He lit them, placed them in various crevices in the cave's walls, then helped Joseph pile straw to make a bed for Mary. It allowed her to sit up yet still recline far enough to relieve the strain on her back. Aaron covered the straw with a blanket. Joseph carried Mary and gently laid her on it. He retrieved a small bundle that held bread and a small amount of cheese, along with the water Caleb had left.

As Mary nibbled the food, the men walked into the night air. Joseph stretched and swung his arms.

"It's been a long day." Aaron twisted his head to loosen the kinks in his neck. "Where do you and Mary live?"

"Nazareth."

"That's at least a six-day journey from here."

Their trip had probably taken several more days. Most Jews coming south would turn west and follow the river to avoid going through Samaria. Samaritans hated Jews. The feeling was mutual. Had they taken the more direct route, Joseph would have probably been robbed and left for dead, and Aaron didn't want to think about Mary's fate. Regardless, with Mary so far along in her pregnancy, it had to have been a hard, long, slow trip.

"Joseph?"

The men turned as Timothy hobbled to where they were standing. "May I go see Mary?"

"If she's awake, it might do her some good to have a little company."

"Be brief," added Aaron. "I need to leave."

The boy smiled and nodded, then disappeared into the stable.

"Could you stay, Aaron?" asked Joseph. "Just long enough for me to wash away some of this dirt. Then maybe I can sleep a little while waiting with Mary."

Aaron understood. Earlier in the day, hadn't he wished to pour a jar of water over his head and sleep for three days? He could only imagine how this man must feel. "Martha should be here soon. Sleep while you can. Mary's not the only one who has a long night ahead."

"Thank you. I won't be long."

When Joseph was out of sight, Aaron returned to the cave. He stopped short when he heard his son speaking to Mary.

"Are you sure you don't mind me being here?"

"I'm glad you came. Where's your father?"

"He's talking with Joseph."

There was a long pause. Aaron wanted to see what was going on, but he remained still.

"Are you scared?" Timothy blurted out the question.

She was silent a moment. "Well, of course. A little. I think every woman about to have a baby is scared. Especially if it's her first time." Mary's voice cracked.

Was that a gasp of pain? Maybe he should fetch Timothy.

"I am scared sometimes."

Aaron stepped back into the shadows. *Timothy—scared?*

"Sometimes at night, I dream that I'm running and playing with my brothers and sisters. Everybody is laughing. My mother and father are there, and they look happier than I've ever seen them. Then I wake up, and nothing's changed."

"And that scares you?"

"No. What scares me is that Mother and Father will never look as happy as they do in my dream."

Aaron thought he'd heard it all when it came to his tiny son. He'd cried tears that he thought would never stop. But never, never, had he felt his heart break as it was doing now.

Before, it was always about himself, about the pain the loss of his son would bring him. Now, hearing Timothy admit he was scared—not for himself, but for his parents—Aaron was ashamed.

Timothy went on. "The rabbi told me that fear is the opposite of faith. Do you believe that?"

Mary was slow to answer. "I suppose. But I also believe that courage is having faith, even when we're afraid."

It was quiet again until Timothy exclaimed, "Look, Mary! A lamb! I wonder where it came from?"

"It was here before we were. Maybe it was scared, and ran into the corner where we couldn't see it."

"It has a funny black spot on its head. Maybe nobody wanted it because it's different. They couldn't sell it, so they just let it go. I think I'm going to ask Father if I can keep it."

Aaron listened. There was a lull in the conversation.

"What are you thinking about?" Mary asked.

Timothy was quiet a moment. "I know how it feels. To be different."

Aaron couldn't stop his tears.

"Timothy, you don't mind that the lamb is different. You see a lamb who needs care. Your family doesn't see you as different, either, but as a beloved child needing special care. It makes you appreciate each other mo—"

Aaron heard a gasp and then a moan.

"Mary!" cried Timothy

Aaron ran into the stable and saw Mary doubled over. Timothy looked terrified.

"Timothy, you need to leave right now. Wait for me outside the stable."

Aaron helped Mary lie back in the crook of his arm for support as he held the water skin for her. "Small sips, Mary. Small sips."

Her face glistened with perspiration.

"I'm going to find Joseph. Martha will be here soon."

Mary looked at Aaron and nodded. She didn't speak, but Aaron felt a churn in his gut. Why?

As he started out of the stable, he heard Timothy yell. Joseph must have started running because he was already at the bottom of the hill when Aaron came out of the cave.

"It's a wonder you didn't break your neck."

Joseph was covered in perspiration. He looked toward the stable.

"She is well, but I need to go find Martha. I think Mary's labor is going to speed up now."

Joseph began to pace.

Aaron stepped in front of him. "Joseph." Aaron placed his hands on the man's shoulders. "Go to Mary. Keep her calm. Martha will be here soon and take care of everything else. I must return to the inn, but will come back as soon as I can."

Joseph just nodded.

Aaron gave him a thump on the back. "How many fathers can say their son was born in a stable?"

With a reassuring smile, he turned. Timothy was waiting for him.

It hit him. Whipping around, Aaron saw Joseph standing in the entrance to the stable. The two men stared at one another. How did Aaron know the child would be a son? The two men held up their hands. It wasn't a wave. It was more of an acknowledgment. Of what, exactly, Aaron wasn't sure, but looking at Joseph, he felt the same twinge of uncertainty he felt earlier in the day.

Maybe the comment was just something he said. A casual remark.

Or was it? Could Timothy be right?

The star twinkled like a thousand sparkling diamonds.

The people who walk in darkness shall see a great light.

He had to get to work.

A light shining down on the people of Galilee and Judea.

Chances were, Ebenezer had already come back to find him not there.

Bethlehem would be the birthplace of a king.

He may not have a job when he arrived.

A child would be born whose name would be called Wonderful Counselor.

If he didn't have a job, what would he do?

The everlasting Father.

How would he feed his family? Pay for Timothy's medicine?

The Prince of Peace.

Aaron looked into his son's face. The child was beautiful in the starlight. Unless one looked below his waist, one would never know anything was wrong. His eyes sparkled, and his smile spread the width of his face. Aaron picked him up and placed him on his shoulders.

Just as they started up the hill, a scream came from within the cave. Aaron looked toward the inn then spun around. There was no longer a question. It didn't matter who the baby was. He set Timothy down and ran to the stable.

★   ★   ★

Aaron wrung the water from the cloth and handed it to Joseph kneeling next to his wife and wiping the cool compress across her forehead.

Martha arrived, taking over and shooing both men from the stable.

Aaron paused, seeing the lamb in the corner. Mary's gaze was fixed on it. He read her lips.

"The Lord is my shepherd—I shall not want."

Another spasm hit, and she moaned.

"Thy rod and thy staff, they comfort me."

Mary cried out.

Time to leave.

Eleven

Ebenezer gasped for air. Someone was suffocating him, cramming something into his mouth. He tried to twist away.

He woke with his head buried in the blanket.

He sat up, and shook his head to clear the mental fog. He walked to the front room. It was still lit by the shaft of starlight shining through the window. He looked around the room at the mess he'd made when Gabriel first appeared. He didn't feel like cleaning it up. It could wait.

Try as he might, Ebenezer could no longer deny what was happening to him. Whether he indulged in too much wine, or suffered hunger or exhaustion, Ebenezer was not only seeing angels, but talking to them. Did he really see the past? His past? Maybe he was just going insane. That would explain it.

Not knowing what else to do, Ebenezer crawled back in bed. Interlacing his fingers behind his head, he tried to remember everything Gabriel said. The thing that puzzled him the most was the nonsense about fulfilling a prophecy. A king being born in his own stable? Impossible. If forced, he could believe the rest of it, but not that. It just couldn't be.

Ebenezer turned on his side, his favorite sleeping position. Maybe he could fall back asleep. He closed his eyes, but as if on springs, they snapped open. He heard the tinkle of his sister's bell. Flipping onto his back, he pulled the covers up so only his eyes were visible.

He waited.

And waited.

Nothing.

Then a mist of light drifted into his room, floating just above the floor. It grew brighter and changed color. Brilliant greens, bold reds, vibrant blues. If he'd not been so frightened, he might have enjoyed it.

The resonance of a man's voice summoned him. "Ebenezer!"

He had no recourse. He carefully stepped into the vapor. It parted and formed a path to the front room. Mesmerized, he was unable to go any further. Though he knew the house to be his, it was totally transformed. It was beautiful.

Lamps were lit and placed throughout the room, revealing walls that were no longer cracked and covered with cobwebs and dust. The tapestries and cushions appeared new. Marble floors and the tiles around the fireplace had been restored to their original beauty. A roaring fire reflected in their sheen.

Scattered around the room were platters piled high with every type of fruit and vegetable imaginable. Some he didn't even recognize. There was venison, poultry, and fish. Ebenezer's mouth watered until he had to wipe the drool away with his sleeve. His stomach roared a plea for a taste of the lavish feast.

But the most incredible sight of all was the figure sitting in its midst. He was the largest man—if he could be so called—that Ebenezer had ever seen. The angel appeared to sit on an invisible chair, and though he seemed friendly, Ebenezer was still afraid.

"You've never seen anyone like me before!" The angel's voice was deep, and his laughter reverberated through the room.

Ebenezer admitted he had not, but still wouldn't look directly at the angel.

"I've been sent here to reveal to you the world in which you live but never see. If it doesn't affect you directly, then it doesn't exist. Why, I sit in front of you now, and you refuse to look at me. You might as well wear the blinders of a plowing ass."

Indignant, Ebenezer forced himself to look directly at the angel. He wore a long robe of green velvet. Like the angel of the past, he wore a gold belt cinched at the waist. His long hair hung loose around his shoulders.

The angel smiled. "You are thinking I don't look like an angel."

Ebenezer stuck out his chin. "How do you know what I'm thinking?"

"Oh Ebenezer, I know *everything* about you." The angel laughed. His entire body shook.

Ebenezer couldn't help himself. He chuckled.

The angel held out his arm. "Touch my robe."

"Wait!" Ebenezer withdrew his hand. "You say we will be in the present?"

"Yes."

"There is someone I'd like very much to see. Can you take me there?"

The angel cocked his head. "You are asking me to take you someplace specific?"

Ebenezer realized he may have overstepped, and taken the angel's kind demeanor for granted.

"I know where you want to go and the person you hope to see. You made your choice a long time ago, Ebenezer. You chose profit and loneliness over love and companionship. It is too late. She is happy. She found what she was looking for. And so did you. Now, touch my robe." The angel lifted his hand so his velvet sleeve hung loose in front of Ebenezer.

The innkeeper had no choice. He reached for the robe.

★   ★   ★

Ebenezer immediately found himself in the middle of the marketplace. Only moments before, he'd been surrounded by a banquet of color and pleasant aromas. Now his stomach turned at the stench of rot and decay. He covered his mouth and nose with his sleeve.

Looking down at the innkeeper, the angel said, "It's interesting. You pass through this place everyday. Why is it that you've never noticed the odor before?"

The angel's observation required no reply. Ebenezer was grateful. Should he remove his sleeve from his face, he would vomit.

Ebenezer had no doubt they were in the present. Bethlehem was filled with people, and Roman soldiers galloped through the streets. There were long lines forming in front of tents, where the descendants of David registered for the Roman census. Most of the people were already poor. Caesar Augustus was going to make it difficult for these people to simply survive.

As on his previous journey, Ebenezer and his traveling companion were invisible. They moved through the crowd with ease. It was near the end of the business day. Carts were being packed, animal stalls were locked, and candles were beginning to appear through the doorways. Ebenezer recognized very few of the people, and could call no one by name. It wasn't because they couldn't hear him, but because he'd never taken the time to learn their names.

The angel said, "You have no knowledge of these people. You walk among them, but never see them."

Everyone seemed to be in an extreme hurry to finish their tasks. Ebenezer pointed this out to the angel. "There are plenty of hours left in the day. They could add to their profits if they would work longer."

"Only you would think that, Ebenezer. These people are in a hurry because they want to be home with their families."

"Yes, but if they worked harder, they could improve their situation." It made perfect sense.

"What they consider wealth cannot be carried in one's pocket."

As if to prove his point, the angel stopped close to a cart where a woman stacked flatbread. Ebenezer thought her old, but when two children ran to greet her, throwing their arms around her legs, she laughed, erasing years from her face.

"You look at poverty as having no money. You view it as a character flaw. But people like this poor woman possess riches that far surpass what you have in your accounts."

The angel turned and walked away without giving Ebenezer time to respond.

Puzzled by the "riches" the old woman possessed, he caught up with the angel just in time to see a woman and child pick up rotting vegetables and fruit from the ground and place them into an old sack. Farther down, men filled a cart with fish and meats reeking from a day under the sun.

"What are they doing with that food? Don't tell me they're going to eat it!" Ebenezer held his nose. "It's disgusting!"

The angel stopped abruptly. "Your disgust is a result of your ignorance." This time the angel looked stern, and there was judgment in his voice.

No matter how friendly and jolly the angel seemed, Ebenezer might want to be careful. If provoked, the large spirit could become quite angry. The innkeeper's trepidation returned.

The angel didn't look at Ebenezer. He just held out his arm. "Touch my robe."

★   ★   ★

Ebenezer stood in front of a very small house. The dark sky framed the glorious star overhead. Its brilliance illuminated the shabbiness of the dwelling.

"I don't recognize this place. Should I know it?"

The angel held out his hand, and Ebenezer touched the soft, green sleeve. They were transported inside.

At first, Ebenezer didn't recognize the family. By their conversation, he soon realized this was Aaron's family. The man himself was nowhere to be found.

Good. That means he's still working. Ebenezer felt the angel's gaze.

Martha filled a basket with various items while giving directions to the children.

One of the girls was determined to have her way. "But, Mother, you need me!"

Martha paused her packing. "What I need is for you to stop pressing me on this. I said no, and I don't want to hear another word. Tonight, your responsibilities are here."

"I just can't believe Ebenezer wouldn't give them a room," Ruth said.

Martha shook her head. "They couldn't pay his price. It's as simple as that."

Ebenezer grew uneasy as she checked the sharpness of two knives, one large, one small. Satisfied, she wrapped them in burlap and carefully placed the roll into her basket.

The door opened, and Aaron entered the room, a small boy perched upon his shoulders. There were cheers and greetings from the family. The room radiated love. It made Ebenezer a little sad. He never realized how lonely it was to go home to an empty house. He'd done it for so long that it was as normal as breathing. Necessary, but requiring no emotion. A ritual with no meaning.

Ruth helped her little brother to a stool, placing his crutch against the wall but still within reach. Martha gave last-minute instructions, then she and Daniel prepared to leave. "Don't forget to say your prayers before eating!"

Timothy spoke up. "I'll say it!"

Everyone stopped what they were doing and bowed their heads.

"Thank You, God, for this food. Thank You for our home and our family. Please take care of Mary and Joseph and the baby. And God? Please help Ebenezer. If this is to be a night for miracles, help him be happy. Help him laugh again."

Because the boy didn't open his eyes, he didn't see the family look up at each other as if thinking, *Only Timothy would request such a thing from God.*

The boy finished his prayer. "God bless us, everyone. Amen."

In unison, the family said, "Amen."

"Amen."

"What was that?" The angel looked down at Ebenezer.

"Nothing." He was embarrassed. "I didn't say anything."

"Oh," said the angel. "I thought you said something."

"You were mistaken. *Shh*. I can't hear."

Aaron pulled Martha aside. "I would have gotten here sooner, but Joseph needed me. Hurry to the stable. Mary's labor is progressing quickly."

Ebenezer questioned the angel—"The stable? *My* stable?"—but received no response.

Martha handed Daniel the basket, and placed a shawl around her shoulders. "Where are you going?"

"I have to get back to the inn," said Aaron. "Ebenezer probably knows I've been gone. I may not have a job before this night is over."

Ebenezer's face grew hot with anger. "You mean to say this man hasn't been at work all this time? Why, I've probably been robbed of every shekel at the inn! Losing his job is going to be the least of his worries. I'll have the man flogged!"

The angel didn't say a word. In fact, he acted as though Ebenezer hadn't even spoken.

Aaron followed Martha through the door. She asked how Timothy was doing. "He looks so tired. It's been a long day for him."

"He was a blessing today. Though he's worn out, he couldn't be happier. He felt needed today. He had a purpose. No medicine can do that." Aaron hesitated. "There's something else."

"Can it wait? I really should be going, and so should you."

"Yes, yes, it can wait."

Martha caught up with Daniel.

Aaron watched until they were out of sight. "Yes, Martha, it can wait. I won't have to be the one to tell you. And I'm glad. You'd never believe me."

Ebenezer asked the angel what Aaron meant, but the angel didn't speak.

Aaron looked at the star. "Dear God, You created this world.

You destroyed it then brought it back to life. You parted the seas and freed Your people. There is nothing You can't do. So I ask you this. Please, God. Save my child. My precious boy, who spreads Your word everywhere he goes. He brings the light of Your love to all those who walk in darkness. He asks nothing for himself—but I'm asking. Spare him. I beg You, don't let my son die."

Aaron hung his head. Tears spattered on the ground. Wiping his face, he returned inside.

Ebenezer watched the family, especially the small boy. "Tell me, angel, does the boy live?"

"The laughter in this house will grow silent."

"Isn't there something they can do?"

"Physicians cost money. 'If he dies, so be it. Let him get on with it!'"

Ebenezer bristled, hearing his own words used against him.

The angel ceased to be the jolly character who first appeared to Ebenezer. There was no disguising the anger in his voice. "Just who do you think you are, that you should say who lives and who dies? Look at that poor man's child! Though his time on this earth is short, his absence will be greatly felt. People will mourn. As for you, Ebenezer, your absence, too, will be greatly felt. People will celebrate."

Ebenezer hung his head at the angel's rebuke. Remorse was an unfamiliar and sickening feeling.

Without another word, the angel held out its sleeve.

★　★　★

Ebenezer stood in a different room. Not shabby, nor elegant. A man sat on a cushion, his head buried in his hands. A woman knelt beside him, attempting to console him.

"Why do you consistently set yourself up for heartache? He's made it clear. He wants nothing to do with us."

The man raised his head. Ebenezer realized he was in his nephew's home.

"Why can't he see I want nothing other than to be a family?"

"You may have to accept that your family will just be the three of us."

Ebenezer looked at the angel. *Three?*

"Maybe he'll change once the baby comes," said the young woman.

Isaac shook his head at his wife. "No. If anything, it will only make the situation worse. He holds me responsible for my mother's death. It will just be a reminder that I lived and she didn't."

Ebenezer screamed, "It's true! You killed her!"

The angel looked at him. "He did no such thing."

"He did! She died trying to bring"—spittle dripped from Ebenezer's lips—"him into the world." He waved his arms at his nephew.

"He had nothing to do with your sister's illness. You blame him because you miss her. But if you'd open your eyes, Ebenezer, you would see she lives on."

He sniffled. "What are you talking about?"

"Your pain has festered into an all-consuming anger. It has hardened your heart to the point that all it does is beat. It is unable to feel joy or happiness. It has forgotten how to love. Wake up, Ebenezer. Look at what's in front of you."

Ebenezer stared at his nephew. He slowly circled the boy. "He has green eyes. My sister had green eyes. And his hair, the color of wheat. The contour of his mouth. And"—Ebenezer squatted in front of Isaac—"the way he holds his head and weeps. I watched his mother do the same. The agony of knowing when something was completely out of her control. Why have I not noticed these things?"

Isaac stood and banged his fists against the wall. "Ebenezer is the only person who can tell me about my mother. There is so much I want to know. What was she like as a child? What made her happy? What was her favorite color?"

Blue. Her favorite color was blue.

The angel towered over Ebenezer. "All this boy wants are answers, yet you refuse to even give him that! You are a self-absorbed, thoughtless, heartless man, Ebenezer. All you do is take. You rob people of their money. You strip away their dignity. You deprive them of happiness. It's time you saw the results of your despicable life. Now come. My time grows short."

The angel didn't wait for Ebenezer's touch.

★　★　★

It was so dark, Ebenezer couldn't see his hand in front of his face. A whoosh of wind swirled around him. Small animals scurried around his feet. Rats. Ebenezer was scared to move for fear of stepping on one or being bitten. Where was he? And where was the giant angel?

"Angel? Where are you? I can't see! What is this place? Please answer me!"

His own voice echoed back to him in mocking reply.

He thought he detected movement ahead. "Angel? Is that you?"

There was definitely something in front of him. Eyes glowed in the dark. There were unidentifiable noises. Where was he? Again, something in front of him scattered. More than one! Oh, where was he? Ebenezer shook uncontrollably. He yelled for the angel to save him, for he knew he would certainly be eaten.

He squinted through the darkness. Was that light ahead? Candles, maybe? He tried to make his way through the dark. He fell, scraping his knees and tearing his robe. He cut his hands trying to break his fall. Hearing a noise, he jumped up, fearing some unseen foe, and continued to shuffle toward the lights.

There it was again. The strange noise.

Ebenezer's senses adjusted. What he thought to be animal noises were actually hushed conversations. And coughing. Terrible fits of hacking and wheezing. There were people in here. And what he had imagined to be the reflections of animals' eyes were actually candles set in the crevices of stone walls. He was in a cave. He moved closer. What he saw was appalling.

He was in a colony of lepers.

He tried to run in the opposite direction. Surely the entrance to the cave was behind him. He stumbled and fell. He saw light ahead, and was able to find the wall of the cave. He clawed his way along.

Emerging from the cavern, he saw that he was in some sort of encampment. Who were these people? They were dressed in rags, and sitting around small fires. Some were roasting an unidentifiable meat on spits made of twigs. Children who looked like skeletons slept next to their parents, covered only by thin, worn blankets. A man pushed a cart through the area, and Ebenezer recognized the cart as one he'd seen earlier being packed with scraps and rotting meat. People pushed and shoved to retrieve what they could.

The smell was so bad that the bile rose in Ebenezer's throat. He leaned over a stone and vomited. When he was able to stand, the angel appeared beside him.

"Where have you been? I called and called. How dare you leave me in such a place! Who are these people? Haven't they got somewhere they can go? It's a disgrace for people to live like this. Eating rotten food, living in caves!"

"'If the poor refuse to avail themselves of the free room and board offered in such places, what business is that of mine? They can sleep in the streets, for all I care!'"

"You mock me. You use my words against me."

"'I pay my taxes. Taxes that help pay for debtors' prisons where the so-called "less fortunate" can go.'"

"I may have misspoken. It doesn't change the fact that my taxes *do* pay for such things. I am certain of it."

"You are ignorant, Ebenezer. You know nothing of these people's suffering."

"I most certainly—"

"Touch my robe."

Ebenezer had barely touched the fabric, yet the field of poverty was gone. In its place was a cave.

The angel didn't look at Ebenezer. He seemed more interested in watching the man who paced back and forth at the entrance to the cave. "Do you recognize this place?"

Ebenezer glanced around. "I can't say that I do."

"You don't even recognize your own stable?"

"If this is my stable, why is that man here? He's trespassing!"

The angel turned to Ebenezer. "Is that what you see? You had no idea this was even your property. Why should you care if he's here?"

"Because it's mine!"

Without warning, Ebenezer was standing at the entrance to the cave.

The innkeeper looked closely at the man. "I recognize him now. He was at the inn today, looking for a room."

"And yet here he is. Outside a stable while his wife is inside, delivering her baby."

"I know nothing about a baby!"

"Would it have made a difference if you did?"

A scream burst from the cave.

"What was that? Was that the woman?"

A woman rushed out of the stable. She handed the man a jar and gestured toward the top of the hill. Ebenezer recognized Martha, Aaron's wife. So this is where she was going. He remembered her leaving with a basket of supplies. He thought of the knives, and suddenly he felt weak.

Ebenezer started to ask the angel about her condition, but he was gone.

The father-to-be passed Ebenezer on the way up the hill. He looked exhausted.

Another cry erupted from the depths of the cave. Ebenezer felt his muscles clench. What was happening in there? Whatever it was, he didn't want any part of it and turned to walk away. He felt his robe tighten, as if caught on something. Turning to release it, he found himself standing next to the angel. He could only see Martha's back, but she knelt in front of the woman giving birth. Ebenezer saw gore-covered rags. The knives, obviously used, lay on the ground. He could smell the coppery odor of fresh blood and wet hay. Martha's robe was soaked in sweat, but all he could see of the woman in labor were her hands stretched out on each side of Martha, clawing and grabbing handfuls of hay as she writhed in pain. Her moans ripped at Ebenezer's heart.

He turned away, and this time made it out of the cave. The echo of an ear-piercing cry followed him.

The angel came walking out of the stable and stood next

to Ebenezer. He remained quiet.

"Has the baby been born? Speak to me! What happened? Don't tell me she—she—"

"Are you asking if she's dead? Does it really matter?"

"I saw the knives, the blood. She seemed in so much pain."

"'Let them go bed down with the sheep for all I care!' Well, here they are, Ebenezer. Right where you sent them."

"Is this the prophecy Gabriel talked about?"

The large angel looked down at the man, but remained silent.

"I realize I may have made a poor judgment by not giving this couple a room, but—"

"But what?"

"I refuse to believe that woman is giving birth to the Son of God. I don't know what kind of game you and your kind are playing, but I've had enough. God's Son! You must think me mad!" Ebenezer was so enraged, he spit saliva with every word.

"I don't think you mad, Ebenezer. I think you pathetic."

Thunder rumbled, and lightning split the sky. It revealed the two travelers were standing in a barren field. The wind howled, and Ebenezer's night clothes whipped around him. His oily, matted hair blew across his face.

"Look here, Ebenezer!" The angel's voice boomed over the storm.

The man was so frightened he stood as close to the angel as possible. He detected movement beside him. The angel parted the flaps of his robe. Underneath, a pair of wings folded across the front, hiding what Ebenezer assumed to be the angel's legs.

The wings parted and spread open to form a shelter over two children. Both were emaciated, their bones protruding under grey skin. Ebenezer gasped.

"Who are these children? Do they belong to you?" He was appalled.

Lightning spread like veins across the field.

"They are yours, Ebenezer. The boy is Ignorance. The girl is Want. You've helped give birth to them both. It will be up to you if they live or die."

Ebenezer recoiled when the two children raised their eyes to meet his. "Cover them. I do not wish to see them."

The angel did so. "Regardless whether or not you see them, they live. Yes, Ebenezer. They do live! And their fate is in your hands."

"But you said I had no right to decide who lives and who dies."

"You have no right, yet you choose, nonetheless. You embrace control, but are blind to its consequences."

The angel began to disappear.

Somewhere in the distance, a bell rang. It wasn't the sweet tinkle of his sister's bell. This was a foreboding sound. Ebenezer panicked. He ran after the angel.

"Please, don't leave me here! I'm lost! How do I find my way home? Help me!"

A tremendous flash of light spread across the sky. Ebenezer saw a figure in the distance. Fear engulfed him as he realized it must be his next traveling companion. He begged for mercy. The closer the draped figure came, the more Ebenezer sobbed. He crumpled to the ground and lost consciousness.

Twelve

After watching Daniel and Martha set off for the stable, Aaron spent a few moments with the rest of his family before rushing back to work. Everything seemed in order. Almost all the guests were asleep, and those who weren't didn't want to be disturbed.

Aaron leaned against the inn's doorframe, studying the sky. *"The people who walk in darkness shall see a great light."*

He glanced across the market to the well. Without the crowd, there was nothing to obstruct his view. He was waiting. Unless something had already happened, eventually the man would show. Then Aaron could clear his head once and for all. He was exhausted. The last thing he needed was to be conflicted about some ridiculous notion. Since his conversation with Timothy, Aaron had been going over and over everything he knew about the scriptures and what they say about the arrival of the Messiah.

A *baby? The Savior of the world? Impossible. But what was it that Timothy said? Micah. It had to do with Micah.*

Aaron carried a lamp back to Ebenezer's private room and removed the wineskin from its hiding place. Everything remained quiet, so he carried it across the market and sat on the wall adjacent to the well. He uncapped the top and took a long drink.

The star was so large, so bright, that it spanned the night sky, obliterating any other heavenly body. *"A great light will shine down on the people of Judea and Galilee."*

Aaron took another sip of the wine, and held it in his mouth to savor the flavor. *What a difference.* More proof of just how awful the wine served at the inn really was. He knew he should feel badly about taking the wine from Ebenezer's room, but considering what the man had put him through, Aaron felt justified.

"And the child's name would be Wonderful Counselor, the Mighty God—"

Aaron looked around. If someone saw him sitting on the wall alone, drinking wine and talking to himself, they'd think him drunk or crazy.

Aaron turned sideways and lay on his back along the top of the wall. The stones dug into his skin, but being off his feet and lying down felt wonderful. He stared at the sky.

Micah. What did he say about Micah?

"Aaron?"

He sat up. "At last."

Joseph set down the empty jar he'd just carried up the hill. "What are you doing here?"

"Waiting for you."

"But, how did you know I'd be here?" Joseph accepted the wineskin Aaron handed over.

"Remember, I've been through this before." Aaron nodded toward the water jar. "So, how many times have you climbed that hill?"

Joseph laughed. "Three. The first two were legitimate. But this one—" He shrugged, "I was in the way."

Fatigue lined Joseph's face. Maybe this wasn't the best time to talk to him about Timothy.

Joseph took a sip of wine. "Mmm. You didn't get this at the inn."

"That's exactly where I got it."

"Won't Ebenezer miss it?"

"He won't mention it, because he won't remember how much he drank. Besides, I saw his robe when he left. He was *wearing* a lot of what used to be in that skin."

Joseph smiled. Aaron thought that a good sign. Nothing unusual going on.

Both men were quiet, enjoying the wine, the starlight, and the peacefulness of the uninterrupted quiet. There were people around them, leaning against building walls, and stretched on pallets in alleyways. Almost all were asleep. A few unintelligible whispered conversations broke the silence every now and then, but other than that, the two men seemed utterly alone.

Aaron asked about Mary.

"Martha assures me things are progressing as they should. But—" Joseph took another sip of wine and handed the skin back to Aaron. He leaned his back against the wall.

Aaron capped the wineskin and set it aside. "When Martha had Daniel, I was like you. I couldn't fathom that kind of pain. And I was sent on needless errands, but they didn't include making a trek up the hill from a stable."

The men grew quiet again. Aaron kept his eyes out for anyone coming or going from the inn. He wasn't about to leave again until he could be relieved, but he wasn't going to miss this opportunity to talk to Joseph, either. He needed to clear this Messiah thing up once and for all. He just didn't know how to broach the subject.

"Aaron?"

"Yes?"

"Why did you say that my *son* would be born in a stable?"

Aaron hesitated. "Who knows? Maybe you'll have a girl."

"No. It's going to be a boy."

Aaron began to get that feeling in his gut. "How can you be so sure?"

"I just know."

"Have you decided on a name?"

"Jesus. His name will be Jesus." Joseph walked away from Aaron and looked at the sky.

Aaron decided to jump right in. He could lose the opportunity at any moment. "We were walking down the hill, and Timothy began quoting scriptures."

"Which scriptures?" Joseph didn't turn around.

Aaron swallowed. "Well, at first it was Isaiah. About a great light shining down on the people of Judea and Galilee. I guess he was thinking the star was the great light. I don't know. His imagination gets carried away sometimes, or he reads things into situations that aren't there."

"Anything else?" Joseph remained still.

"He mentioned Micah."

Joseph looked at Aaron. "Bethlehem will be the birthplace of a king."

Aaron's mouth went dry. His tongue felt glued to his teeth. He reached for the wineskin and took a drink. Then one more.

Joseph sat on the wall, leaving plenty of room between the two men.

"As I'm sure you've noticed, I'm considerably older than Mary. I wasn't sure I'd remarry after my first wife died, but because of my friendship with Mary's father, I've known Mary for years. I saw her often. After several months, it was arranged that we'd wed.

"I was fortunate. Mary seemed to care deeply for me, and we were happy. We became closer as time went on, and

90

were looking forward to when our union was official. Then everything changed." Joseph rubbed his temples.

"About six months ago, Mary came to me. She'd been gone for almost three months to visit her cousin Elizabeth. When she arrived home, we took a walk, just the two of us. That's when she told me she was going to have a baby. Since we'd not been together in that way, you can imagine what I thought." Joseph's voice cracked.

He gestured to Aaron he'd like a sip of wine. Handing over the wineskin, Aaron kept quiet. Returning it, Joseph continued.

"I demanded to know who the father was. What she told me was absurd. I couldn't believe she'd blaspheme in such a way. Maybe she'd been attacked by a soldier and suppressed the memory."

Aaron finally interrupted. "Just what was it she said?"

"An angel told her she would have a Son, conceived by the Holy Spirit, and He would be the Savior of the world. She even told me His name. What was I to think?"

Aaron remained silent.

"The more Mary insisted the story to be true, my thoughts turned ugly. I accused her of protecting the man's identity. That the only reason she'd spent so long visiting her cousin was to be with him."

His voice caught, as if he relived the anguish.

"According to our laws, once Mary and I were betrothed, if I were to die, she would receive everything I own. But after she became pregnant, the same law said I had the right to either have her stoned or have her banished in shame. So I prayed." Joseph scoffed. "I prayed God would tell me which of those two choices was best." He dropped the bucket into the well, then drew it up again and set the dripping bucket on the low stone wall around the well. "If she'd just tell me the truth, I could forgive her. Instead, she kept repeating the same story."

"What did you decide?"

"I would send her away. I mean, who would make up such a story? So, instead of Mary being labeled an adulteress, I would protect her and let people think her crazy instead."

Joseph cupped his hands and splashed water on his face.

Aaron's thoughts spun. None of this could be real. He must be more exhausted than he thought. He'd fallen asleep, and this was a dream. The Messiah was being born this night in Bethlehem, in a stable where Aaron had sent them, and he was alone with the child's earthly father, hearing a firsthand account of how it all happened? Yes. He had to be dreaming.

"Please," said Aaron, "give me a moment to gather my thoughts."

Joseph splashed more water on his face, rubbed his eyes, ran his fingers through his thick hair and dark beard, then used his robe as a towel.

Aaron took a deep breath and slowly released it. He looked at Joseph. "You didn't send Mary away."

"I love her, Aaron. With all of my heart. That's why the decision was so painfully difficult. I knew Mary wasn't crazy. I didn't believe she would have committed adultery, either. And I refused to believe that she'd blaspheme. Not Mary. It's against her nature."

"So, how did you make your decision?"

"It turns out, I didn't have to choose."

"Why?"

"The angel came to me, too. He told me to believe every word Mary said."

Aaron jumped off the wall and dropped the wineskin to the ground. He paced in a tight circle, then stopped and stood in front of Joseph.

Joseph half-smiled. "You don't believe me."

"I didn't say that."

"I wouldn't blame you. It's still hard for me to grasp the magnitude of it."

Aaron walked a distance away and stared at the sky. "If what you're telling me is true, that *your* son is *God's Son*, then that means my family and I are part of the story." He shook his head and sighed. "Timothy put it all together. He tried to explain it to me, but I didn't want to believe it. I was worried what you might think of him should he say anything, so I asked him to keep it to himself. It's strange. We're always so quick to brag about our children if they've done something that makes us proud. The truth of it is, parents often brag because it makes *us* look good. But when the child does something questionable or wrong, we try to hide it, keep it to ourselves. We don't want it to reflect that we're bad parents."

"It's obvious you and Martha are great parents."

"We do the best we can. It hasn't always been easy. When Timothy was born, things were difficult. Sleepless nights, his constant care, my work and the small income—hardly a day went by that Martha and I didn't argue. The more we fought, the more the children fought, and Martha and I couldn't even agree on how to discipline them. Our entire household was in chaos."

"So what changed? How did you get through it?"

Aaron softly chuckled. "Prayer and patience. Though it was slow and is still painful at times, bit by bit we became better. Love is stronger than hateful words."

The men were quiet until Joseph asked, "Aaron?"

Aaron returned to the wall. "Yes?"

"How do I be a father to God's Son?"

Aaron hesitated. "Hmm. A formidable position. If God entrusted His Son to your care, He must believe you're up to the task. And who knows you better than the One who created you?"

"Yes, but *what* do I teach Him?"

"Well, I guess you teach Him what any good father teaches his son."

"It can't be that simple."

"Why not? He'll need to be taught the laws of Moses. How to respect His elders, hold His temper, to show compassion and forgiveness." Aaron shook his head. "Those are the ones that give my family the most trouble. Holding our temper and forgiving those who don't deserve it. Hardly a day goes by that I don't have to deal with Ebenezer's selfish behavior. I can usually let it go, but some days it is a terrible struggle not to strike back. We'll be out with Timothy, and somebody's child will make fun of him. Our children want to retaliate. I'll admit, I struggle with forgiveness. It's not an easy lesson to teach or learn."

Joseph remained quiet.

"He may be God's Son, Joseph, but God has placed Him in your hands. If God doesn't question your abilities, then you certainly shouldn't. You can teach Him to be a carpenter."

"How did you know I was a carpenter?"

"Timothy told me. He—"

The sky exploded with light. The great star erupted into millions of cascading crystals, so bright the men had to shield their eyes. They heard singing from somewhere in the distance.

The two men looked at one another then ran down the hill.

Aaron never looked back toward the inn. It no longer mattered, because there was no doubt.

The Messiah had been born.

Thirteen

Ebenezer opened his eyes. He tried to sit up, but he was cold, and his body ached. Heavy, wet clothes clung to his body. He had no sense of time. He remembered how bright things were when the large star illuminated the sky, but now there was no light at all.

He detected movement somewhere in the darkness. He clumsily tried to stand, stumbled, and banged his head on a rock. A drop of warm, sticky liquid slid down his cheek, and he knew it was blood. Something was close by, and he trembled, waiting for it to show itself.

The blackness swayed, and Ebenezer realized it was the cloak of the dark figure he'd seen before. He fell to his knees. "Mercy."

He saw no face within the folds of fabric, as if the hood protected black air. The angel made no sound. In his attempt to stand, Ebenezer held out his hand for assistance but received no aid.

"I have been with two of your brothers. They have shown me my past and present life. Am I to assume you are here to show me my future?"

The angel gave no response. It merely held out its arm.

It unnerved Ebenezer to think that eyes he couldn't see were staring at him. "Will you not speak to me?"

Realizing no conversation would be forthcoming, the innkeeper said, "Lead on then."

The angel's sleeve still hung in front of Ebenezer. He reached out and touched it. Immediately he was engulfed in mist, and when it cleared, he stood in a large hall. The polished marble floor reflected the ornate ceiling and walls covered in gold, ivory, and tapestries of textured silk.

Several men stood together, hunched over a table, intently reading and securing the charts and scrolls spread across it. From the color of their skin and form of dress, Ebenezer surmised they were of Eastern descent. Servants carried platters piled with delectable fruits, cheese, meats, and bread. Others brought wine in goblets of gold inlaid with precious jewels. The men, however, were engrossed in conversation about the documents on the table.

Suddenly, the servants dropped to the floor. Ebenezer was shocked. In walked King Herod. He clapped, and all the servants quickly retreated, leaving only the guests and a few of the king's advisors.

Herod smiled, motioning to the feast and encouraging his guests to make themselves comfortable. Again, the men seemed more interested in their charts than eating. A look of annoyance flashed across the king's face.

"Tell me more about this King of the Jews."

Ebenezer moved closer. *King of the Jews?*

One of the men spoke. "We have been following the star for almost two years. It's been on a steady western course. In the past few months, it's gained in speed and size."

Another man tried to show a chart to Herod, who pushed it away. Instead, he poured wine and said, "Go on."

"The star has slowed again and changed course. It's headed south."

The king circled the men. He reminded Ebenezer of a beast ready to pounce.

"So you're convinced the star will lead you to this—" It seemed Herod couldn't even speak the word.

"We have studied for years, preparing for this event. The signs have fallen into place. The star is leading us to the child."

"What?" Herod wheeled around so fast that his wine sloshed on the floor. He slammed the goblet on the table. "Child? You didn't mention he was a baby."

"We can't be certain of the child's age. We only know that his birth should—or would—have taken place about this time."

Herod paced back and forth. "You have convinced me. This child should be found. I will give you whatever is needed to aid your quest. Please, enjoy the food and a good night's rest. We'll speak again in the morning."

Herod left the room, followed closely by his advisors.

"Aid in their quest! Ha!" Ebenezer looked at the angel by his side. He still couldn't see a face, but had no doubt it could hear his one-sided conversation. "I don't know anything about this child, but whoever he is, he'd better watch out. Herod's not going to sit idly by knowing there may be a threat to his throne!"

The angel held out its sleeve, and the moment Ebenezer touched it, he stood in a smaller version of the room they'd just left. Herod was angry, his eyes mere slits as he glared at the men who were searching for answers. Ebenezer recognized the High Priest and other members of the Sanhedrin.

"Have you found anything yet?" Herod demanded. "Do the prophets mention this King of the Jews?"

"Yes, they do." The chief priest was obviously nervous. He stayed on the opposite side of the table, as far away from the king's reach as possible. "The prophet Micah wrote about a governor being born in Bethlehem who would rule the people of Israel."

Herod was furious. He screamed at a servant to bring him his guests. When the astronomers entered, the irate king's demeanor immediately changed.

"My advisors and priests have been up all night, trying to discern where you might find the child. I believe they may have your answer. Follow your star to the village of Bethlehem. Once you've found the child, come back here. I will be waiting. It is only right that I should go meet the new ruler."

Ebenezer felt uneasy. "He's up to something. He'll stop at nothing to destroy any threat to his power. Even his own family."

He watched the men leave and, as the mist surrounded him, Ebenezer heard Herod call for the head of the Royal Guard.

★　　★　　★

The scene changed, and the invisible pair stood on a hill overlooking a dusty road. The sun was just coming up. The sky was a mixture of red, orange, purple, and blue, and there was a slight breeze spreading the fragrance of wild flowers. Ebenezer inhaled deeply, then slowly released his breath. He did it several times, trying to clear the overwhelming scents of incense, perfumes, and lamp oil that permeated Herod's palace.

Odd. I'm invisible, yet can smell the scents around me.

Ebenezer recognized Bethlehem in the distance. Sheep grazed in the fields beyond the city. The shepherds must be enjoying the beautiful morning. Briefly forgetting the cloaked figure beside him, Ebenezer closed his eyes, and let the breeze caress his face as he listened to the songs of the birds. For a moment, he felt peaceful and serene, sensations that had grown foreign to him.

Something moved beside him, and when he looked, the angel was pointing down the road. A man approached. He led a small donkey carrying a parcel on its back. The closer they came, Ebenezer realized it wasn't a parcel at all, but a woman.

"I recognize that couple. They were in my stable!"

The figure beside him turned. Though Ebenezer couldn't see the angel's face, he felt sure he was being given a look of reproach.

Regardless, he asked, "Where are they going? Is it too soon for the baby and mother to travel?"

No answer.

Ebenezer muttered, "I don't know why I bother asking you anything!"

The angel held out its arm. Annoyed, Ebenezer touched it, and the travelers stood on a different hill, the couple and baby nowhere in sight.

The sky was clear, and the sun straight overhead. He stood on a rise outside Bethlehem, in clear view of the marketplace. There were no soldiers, no peddlers selling their wares. Women gathered around the well, filling jugs, washing clothes, and catching up on news. Men worked, and small children played. He saw the inn, and what he now knew to be his assistant's home. He could see his own house in the distance. Even from where he stood, it appeared a dilapidated, uninhabitable shell.

A low rumble of thunder broke the silence. Ebenezer looked around. It was a beautiful day, without a cloud in the sky. Why would he hear thunder? He shielded his eyes. Sure enough, off to the north, dark clouds were forming and moving rapidly in his direction. They were unlike any he'd ever seen.

Then he knew.

They weren't clouds at all, and the sound wasn't thunder. It was dust and the pounding of galloping horses.

Something horrific was about to happen, and there was nothing he could do about it. He turned to the angel, but before he could utter a word, the pair was standing in front of the inn.

The soldiers sped into Bethlehem, taking the citizens by surprise. Men yelled, women screamed, and children cried out in fear. Soldiers dismounted with swords drawn, and started slaying the ones who had the least chance to get away. The children. It was a massacre.

The soldiers didn't leave a table unturned. Buildings were ransacked, and burned if the soldiers suspected someone was hiding inside. Children were ripped from their mothers' arms. If anyone intervened, they too felt the pain of the soldiers' blood-covered blades.

It was clear. The mission was to kill the children, particularly the boys—but, regardless of age, any small child within reach was butchered.

He tried to help, running through the streets, screaming for people to get out of the way, and pushing children out of the soldiers' reach. It was no use. No one could hear his warnings or see his offer of aid. All he could do was watch in horror.

"Please, please, make it stop!" Ebenezer screamed. "Do something! How can you be from God yet stand there mute and do nothing?"

On his knees, pleading, Ebenezer held his face in his hands, sobbing as the soldiers made one more pass through town. The sound of receding horses was replaced by screams of pain and cries of grief.

As the dust settled, Ebenezer saw more clearly the devastation Herod's soldiers left behind. Many of those he watched were people he'd seen on his previous travels with the angels. The woman who'd been stacking bread, her children hugging her legs, now held her dead son in her arms. Those who, just a short time ago, had been gathered for a family meal, now gathered around a loved one's small lifeless body. Children who were laughing and playing only moments earlier now lay in their own blood, silent and still.

Most of the dead children were males. Ebenezer understood now. Herod's plan was to make sure there was no one to threaten his reign. He was a ruler gone mad.

Those who survived the onslaught attended to those who didn't. As if out of nowhere, bandages, blankets, water, and medicine quickly appeared. A man and woman took charge, and when they turned, Ebenezer was greatly relieved to see Aaron and Martha.

A woman held a hysterical mother cradling a dead child. Ebenezer recognized the first woman. His nephew's wife. Had their baby been born? Had their child died that day? Then he saw Isaac across the square, bandaging the wounds of a man who had tried to stop the slaughter.

Blood pooled where the soldiers' boots and horse hooves had sunk into the dirt. It trickled in rivulets where women had dropped their jars of water. The copper smell of blood filled the air.

Why? Why was he seeing this?

The dark figure beside him held out its arm. As the view receded, the wails in Bethlehem could still be heard.

Fourteen

When the fog cleared, Ebenezer stood outside a house in another village. There was no carnage, no cries for lives lost.

He was outside a shop, and through its open door saw two men standing opposite each other. A log lay between them. In perfect rhythm, they moved back and forth as they shaved the wood to a smooth plank. It reminded Ebenezer of a dance.

A woman arrived with a simple plate of food and a jug of water. As the men ate, she ran her hands over the smooth piece of wood. She smiled. That's when Ebenezer recognized her. The woman who bore her baby in his stable.

Ebenezer studied the two men. The older man appeared to be the baby's father. Could that mean the younger man was the baby, all grown up? By the looks of his parents, he would be about the right age. If so, Gabriel was wrong. This man was just a carpenter, not a leader of Israel. Ebenezer felt a pang of disappointment.

I almost hoped you were the king. That would mean Herod failed, and those children didn't die for nothing.

★　　★　　★

Mist rose, and the carpenter's shop disappeared. When the fog cleared, Ebenezer stood on a hillside amidst hundreds of other people: men, women, old, young. Some looked the picture of health, while others appeared to be at death's door. Some in the crowd looked wealthy, while others seemed to carry all of their possessions in the bag by their side. All they had in common was their focus on the man standing in the distance.

Ebenezer squinted. "Are we here because of that man?"

Receiving no answer, he became agitated.

"How can I know why we're here, and what I'm to gain from it, if you refuse to speak to me?"

The angel's response was to hold out its sleeve. Ebenezer cursed but touched it, and was instantly in front of the speaker. It was the man who, only moments before, had been helping his father in the wood shop.

The angel gave him no direction not to, so Ebenezer sat down.

The man's voice was strong yet comforting. Though the crowd was spread over a large area, everyone seemed able to hear. His voice, his eyes, the way he used his hands, all worked to captivate his audience.

Ebenezer looked around. He couldn't imagine what a simple carpenter would have to say that was so important as to draw such a crowd. He began to listen.

"If you hunger and thirst for all that is good, you will be filled. Those who show mercy shall receive mercy. Like a city on a hill sheds its light throughout the darkness, you can be a guiding light for others. Do not worry about situations that occur in life. Instead, pray about them, and leave the results to God. Worry doesn't solve anything."

Ebenezer was confused. He followed what the man was saying, yet who was he to be teaching it? The carpenter was no scholar, no priest. Yet for one who appeared so humble, he spoke with great authority.

The man taught about anger, murder, revenge, and prayer, but when he told the crowd to love their enemies, Ebenezer jumped up. Until that moment, he'd been intrigued. Love one's enemies?

"Ha!" Ebenezer cursed.

The angel appeared, and mist surrounded them. As it began to encircle Ebenezer, he looked back at the teacher, and could have sworn the man was looking at him. Impossible. He was invisible. Nevertheless, it was unsettling.

★　★　★

Ebenezer began a whirlwind of encounters with the man. Time after time, the angel took him to places where the carpenter was teaching. Sometimes the crowd was large. Other times, he sat in on intimate conversations. Ebenezer enjoyed these occasions the most. Whether at a home, sharing a meal, or in a garden with the twelve men who traveled with the teacher, the more Ebenezer listened, the more he liked the man.

As a child, Ebenezer had loved to read. It was how he comforted himself when spending so much time alone. The stories became his friends. Maybe that's why he enjoyed listening to the carpenter. He taught by telling stories and parables. They were lessons on how to live a happier, more productive life. Ebenezer didn't always agree with the rabbi, or follow his logic, but he was still intrigued.

Not everyone approved of what the man said. One such group was the Pharisees, who made it their mission to trouble the young teacher.

On one occasion, as Ebenezer walked beside the carpenter, one of the pious leaders stopped to question him: "Which of God's commandments do you think to be the most important?"

Ebenezer told the angel, "He's baiting him!"

The teacher didn't hesitate. "Love the Lord your God with all your heart, soul, and mind. This is the first and greatest commandment. The second is similar. Love your neighbor as yourself. Keep these two, and you will obey all the others."

Ebenezer nodded in approval—*Good answer*—but he knew that wasn't the end of it. The men would try again.

It didn't take long.

One day he watched the Pharisees push a woman to the ground in front of the rabbi.

"She was caught in the sin of adultery. The Law of Moses says she is to be stoned! What do you say?"

The teacher knelt down and drew in the dirt. Ebenezer couldn't tell if he was writing something profound or just scribbling. Maybe he was taking his time to formulate his answer, to keep his composure, or to simply make the Pharisees squirm. It didn't matter. Ebenezer couldn't wait to hear the rabbi's reply.

The teacher slowly stood. He looked at the woman on the ground then faced the men. "You're right. That is what the scriptures say. So go ahead and stone her. But—"

Ebenezer grinned. *Here it comes!*

"—the one who has never sinned be the one to throw the first stone."

The men walked away, muttering among themselves. Ebenezer wanted to applaud. He surmised the Pharisees were already scheming. They had no intention of letting Rabbi— Ebenezer realized he didn't even know the man's name.

He watched as the teacher knelt, brushing the hair out of the woman's face. He asked where her accusers were. She looked around. He helped the woman to her feet, said that no one had judged her and she should go and live a life free of shame and sin. She appeared uncertain, but as she walked away, she kept turning back. Each time, she looked younger, happier. She held her head high. She was free.

As the rabbi turned to resume his walk, he looked at Ebenezer. It happened every time the innkeeper was in the man's presence. Ebenezer shivered. Could the man see him? There were even times when Ebenezer thought the teacher was speaking specifically to him.

"The more lowly your service to others, the greater you are. To be the greatest, be a servant. Those who think themselves great shall be disappointed and humbled, and those who humble themselves shall be exalted."

Ebenezer studied the man. He certainly practiced what he preached. After all, he was a simple carpenter. And though a poor man, he never seemed without friends and followers. He seldom went without food, and was as content to sleep under the stars as he was in a bed.

★　★　✱

The day finally came when Ebenezer learned the teacher's name. Even before the mist cleared, Ebenezer could hear music.

The angel had taken him to a wedding. The celebration was lively, and everyone was enjoying the festivities. The rabbi was there, along with the same group of men who followed him everywhere.

A woman appeared out of the crowd, drawing the man's attention. Ebenezer recognized her. It was the man's mother, and she called her son by name. "Jesus."

Keeping her voice low, she said, "Our friends have run out of wine. They need your help."

Jesus stepped back and tenderly told her no.

Ebenezer was a bit surprised. He didn't understand why Jesus refused to buy his friends wine. He could have at least asked one of his followers to do it. What's more, the rabbi's mother ignored Jesus' response.

His mother called the servants over and, pointing to Jesus, told them to do whatever he said.

Jesus looked around the room. He pointed to six large barrels standing in the corner of the room, and instructed the servants to fill each one to the top with fresh water. Once they did, he told one of the servants to dip some into a goblet for the master of ceremonies.

When the man tasted it, he exclaimed, "This is wonderful!" He turned to the bridegroom. "Usually the host will serve his best wine at the beginning of a party, saving the less expensive wine for when the guests can no longer tell the difference. You've saved the best for last!"

Ebenezer was dumbfounded. Was the man drunk? He couldn't believe people were going to fall for such nonsense. He turned to the angel, ready to blast the antics, only to find the angel pointing at the drums.

"What is he talking about? I watched those men. They filled those barrels with water!"

The angel remained mute, and continued to point at the large jars.

Ebenezer peeked into the container. It was dark, so he couldn't tell the color of the liquid, yet it smelled like wine. The angel continued to point. If he tasted the liquid, it would be the first time he'd actually participated in the world he was observing.

He dipped a cup into the barrel, then took a sip of the best wine he'd ever tasted. Amazed and bewildered, Ebenezer looked at Jesus. The teacher was smiling, talking with friends and tapping his foot in time to the music, as if oblivious to the miracle.

Ebenezer whirled to face the angel. "You can't fool me! There was wine in those barrels all along. Do you take me for a fool? I won't stand for it!"

He threw down the cup and headed for the door. Tears stung his eyes. He felt betrayed. Ebenezer had grown to like the man. He was beginning to understand what he had to say. Without rubbing his nose in his past, the rabbi made him want a better future. More than anything else, and even though Jesus couldn't see him, Ebenezer felt he had a friend for the first time since childhood.

As he was about to walk out, Ebenezer took one last look at Jesus. There was no doubt the man was looking back. Though Jesus never opened his mouth, Ebenezer distinctly heard him ask, "Do you believe in me?"

Ebenezer hung his head. When he walked out the door, he was engulfed in mist.

Fifteen

Turning water into wine was just the beginning. Time after time, the angel took Ebenezer to watch Jesus perform another miracle. Blind men saw, the sick were restored to health, the lame walked, and even the dead returned to life. Men, women, children, Romans, or Jews—it didn't matter. Jesus treated them all. He healed their bodies and restored their souls, all without fanfare or money exchanging hands.

Try as he might to resist believing otherwise, Ebenezer realized the miracles were not tricks or sorcery. They were real. But that's as far as it went. Most of the people whose lives had been touched believed Jesus to be the Son of God. Ebenezer, however, still refused the notion. The scriptures were full of miracles that didn't require God to be present. Besides, God wouldn't travel masquerading as some poor carpenter.

Though Ebenezer enjoyed the time he spent with the teacher, he still had no idea why he was privy to the man's life. Ebenezer thought his journey with the angel was to see his own future. So far, they'd only focused on Jesus.

Standing in a crowded room, Jesus had just healed a man who'd been lowered through the roof by some friends. The angel appeared ready to depart, but Ebenezer didn't touch the outstretched sleeve. He was intrigued that men would go to such extremes to see their sick friend healed. Friendship was very important to Jesus, and he frequently told stories that emphasized its significance. Ebenezer had no friends. Having friends meant being a friend. He would have to invest in a person, not in the person's purse.

There was another reason Ebenezer paused before leaving the scene. It happened every time he witnessed a miracle: As he was about to touch the angel's sleeve, Jesus would look at him and—without moving his lips, without anyone else hearing—would ask, "Do you believe in me?"

★   ✱   ✻

The mist cleared, and Ebenezer and the angel stood in Aaron's home. The mood was nothing like before. There was no laughter, no animated conversation. The boys were reading, the girls were baking, and Martha sat on a bench, sewing.

Martha dropped her work in her lap, and covered her face with her hands. "The smoke is burning my eyes." After a few deep breaths, she resumed her work. "They're better now."

One of the daughters wiped away a tear then continued her chores.

Martha looked around the room. "I wouldn't want your father to see me this way. He's suffering enough as it is. Ebenezer has given him no time to rest. In fact, Ebenezer has given Aaron more responsibility but less time to accomplish it, and criticizes his every move. I don't know how much more your father can take."

Ebenezer felt his face grow hot.

"Father's strong." Daniel put down his book and walked behind his mother. "He'll be all right. It's just going to take time." He leaned over and gave Martha a kiss on the cheek.

The door opened and Aaron walked in. Ebenezer barely recognized his assistant. His face was drawn and pale. His eyes were dull and sunken, surrounded by dark circles. He'd lost weight, and his clothes hung on him like a loose sack. Nobody spoke. Martha stood and pulled her husband into her arms. Aaron buried his face against her neck.

Finally, he stepped back and wiped his eyes. He sat down as one of the girls poured wine and handed the cup to Aaron.

"I promised him we wouldn't be sad. That was his greatest fear. He never wanted us to forget all the good times we had together. He said to focus on those memories, and to always remember that he's no longer sick, there's no pain, and most importantly, he can walk. Run if he wants."

Aaron rose, and picked up the crutch that had been leaning against the wall. "He told me I should get rid of this—he wouldn't need it anymore—but I can't bring myself to do it." The tears still came. "I know he's better off, but I miss him."

The room was quiet except for the grieving family's weeping.

Caleb spoke up. "I think Timothy laughed more in the short time he was here than most people laugh in their lifetime. He once told me that God must have a great sense of humor."

"What?" Martha blew her nose, and the tears subsided for the rest of the family, too. "What did he mean by that?"

"If we're made in God's image, then He must have a sense of humor," replied Caleb. "It's natural for people to smile and laugh. We're not taught how to do it. Timothy figured it was an instinct God thought important enough to make a part of who we are. I tried to tell him that not everybody smiles and laughs."

"Like Ebenezer!" the youngest daughter spoke up.

"Timothy believed something bad must have happened to Ebenezer, and by shutting everybody out of his life, he's protecting himself from getting hurt again," said Martha. "Timothy said that's why he doesn't smile. He's uncomfortable around joy."

Aaron added, "Timothy had a sense for reading people. He was right. The only relationship Ebenezer has is with his money. It can't break his heart."

Something on Ebenezer's face tickled, like a bug crawling down his cheek. Wiping his fingers across it, he realized it was a tear.

Aaron looked around at his family. "Timothy wouldn't want us to wallow. He'd want us to celebrate every moment we share together. It doesn't mean life will be easy, or that we won't have our share of trials. It means that we'll never go though them alone."

Ebenezer studied the family. They'd spoken of him and his miserable outlook on life, yet he wasn't offended. It was a strange feeling. They'd lost so much, yet they'd lost nothing at all. They were a family in mourning, sustained by what had united them all along.

The angel held out its arm.

"What is left to learn? I don't need any more lessons. I've experienced every possible emotion. Please take me home."

The angel didn't waver. It continued to extend the draping black fabric.

Having no choice, Ebenezer was forced to leave the intimate gathering behind.

★ ✳ ✳

Ebenezer was vomiting, choking on sea water. His body was slammed side to side in a fishing boat in the middle of a torrential storm. Rain pelted him, and lightning streaked across the sky. Wind shredded the sails, and water poured over the sides, filling the boat. The next lightning bolt illuminated the sky, and Ebenezer realized the panicking men were the ones who followed Jesus. They scrambled around Ebenezer, bailing water, trying to keep the the boat from capsizing. It was hopeless. They were sinking.

Gripping the side of the boat, Ebenezer could barely see through the torrents of water. The boat was pitching back and forth, and spinning in the waves. He tried to find the angel, but couldn't see the dark figure in the ferocious storm.

This was it. The angel was going to let him die.

Two of the men crawled to the back of the boat, shaking what appeared to be a pile of canvas tarps. Lightning streaked across the sky, and Ebenezer saw Jesus' face. He'd been asleep! How could anyone sleep through such pandemonium? It was impossible.

Jesus stood, perfectly balanced despite the boat being violently tossed, plunging deep into the waves then hurling back up on a tower of foam. Ebenezer tried to wipe his eyes, but when he let go of the side, he was slapped by a mountain of water and flung overboard. He was immediately swallowed up in the churning water. His tunic wrapped around his arms and legs, pulling him under. His lungs screamed for air. He was going to die. He quit fighting, and surrendered to the sea.

But then a hand grabbed his own. He held on tightly, knowing his life depended on it. At last his head broke through the water. Coughing and spitting, Ebenezer gasped for air. Lightning lit up the sky, and he saw the face of his rescuer. Jesus was looking down at him. The other men were oblivious as they continued to scream.

All at once, all sound ceased. The world around them faded. There was no storm, no people. All Ebenezer could see was Jesus' face, and he could feel the strong hand gripping him. He stared into the rabbi's eyes. He heard the voice. He heard the question.

"Do you believe in me?"

Jesus pulled Ebenezer into the boat, which resumed its vicious rocking. Jesus stood and, holding up his hand, commanded the wind and rain be still. The sea obeyed. It was calm, and the roaring gale became a gentle breeze. The dark sky was illuminated by millions of twinkling, silver stars.

Jesus watched the men respond to the tranquil surroundings. "Why are you afraid? Do you still not have faith in me?"

One by one, the men knelt in front of their master. Jesus stared over their heads at Ebenezer. Neither man said a word. The angel appeared, suspended over the water in a cloudy mist. His black cloak waved, waiting for Ebenezer's touch, but the innkeeper kept his gaze locked on Jesus. He felt an invisible embrace, and heard the holy man speak.

"What do you fear, Ebenezer?"

Sixteen

ven before the mist cleared, Ebenezer heard the roar of the crowd. He was pushed and shoved from every direction. Elbows and hands punched him, spinning him and finally knocking him down. He tried to get up, but had nothing to hold on to. He attempted to grab someone's leg, but was kicked away. He landed on his stomach, his face pressed next to a pile of steaming horse manure. His hands were bleeding from trying to break the fall, and now were being mashed under people's feet. Swearing, Ebenezer was sure several of his fingers were broken.

He finally spotted a wall and tried to crawl toward it, maneuvering his way through the web of legs and feet. He managed to pull himself up, his back flat against the stones. All he could see were waves of heads, necks, and shoulders. The angel was nowhere in sight.

Ebenezer waited until there was a tiny break in the crowd. He lunged forward, and let the sea of humanity carry him up the street. He finally spotted the angel hovering over a stone wall. The being made no effort to help the innkeeper. Instead, he waited, and let the people push Ebenezer to him.

"So nice to see you again."

The angel ignored the sarcastic remark. Instead, he held out his sleeve.

As soon as Ebenezer touched it, he was sitting on top of the wall so he could see the other side. He surveyed his surroundings, and instantly recognized the city of Jerusalem. The streets overflowed with people. From his vantage point, Ebenezer was able to observe one of the many temple courtyards where greedy men exchanged money and sold animals for exorbitant fees. He knew it well. He'd made quite a hefty profit from his dealings there.

"Still at it, I see. How much will you make today? Thieves and cheats, all of you." Ebenezer had yet to see the angel's face, but the draped figure turned toward him, and he sensed the silent rebuke. He felt ashamed. Ebenezer continued to watch the deceitful transactions, and it surprised him how disgusted he felt.

Looking across the rooftops, Ebenezer realized that Jerusalem was truly an architectural marvel. The marble stone of the temple and royal palace sparkled in the sunlight. The house of the ruling High Priest was next to the palace on the south side, and the Roman governor lived at the north end of the temple. A crowd had gathered in the governor's courtyard.

"What's going on? Most Jews avoid the Roman leaders as often as possible, so it must be important for them to gather there." Then he realized he was foolishly explaining information to the angel.

Without warning, Ebenezer stood in the middle of the onlookers. He turned to the angel, but once again found himself alone.

There had to be some mistake.

There, in front of him, was Jesus. But this was not the man he'd walked with, listened to, and watched perform miracles.

Not the one who tapped his foot to music, or bounced children on his knee.

This man was barely able to stand. His clothes—what was left of them—were tattered and covered with blood. There were gashes and bruises on every exposed part of his body, and his right eye was swollen shut. His lips were cracked and caked with blood. What made him all the more pathetic was a prickly vine had been laced into a circle and pressed onto Jesus' head in mocking semblance of a crown. The thorns dug into his scalp, and blood oozed through his oily, tangled hair and slid down his face like red tears.

"Oh my God! What is happening? Why are they doing this?"

A soldier pushed Jesus forward, knocking him to the ground. Ebenezer gasped in horror when he saw the man's back.

"No! No! No!"

Ebenezer had heard about it, but never seen its effects before. Yet there was no doubt in his mind. Jesus had been scourged. Who would demand such torture, and why?

The instrument used was called a flagrum. Leather straps attached to a short handle were tied through sharp sheep bones and balls of lead. When used, the straps would cut the skin while the sharper objects raked the flesh open, shredding it when the lash was withdrawn. It was an inhumane punishment, even for the worst criminals.

Hebrew law restricted the number of lashes to forty, but the Pharisees in their pious grandeur had reduced the number to thirty-nine. They wanted to make sure the torture didn't kill a prisoner. They wanted him alive to rot in prison, to be stoned to death—or, worse, to be crucified by the Romans.

Even if the angel had been standing next to him, Ebenezer wouldn't have been able to say a word. The scene was repugnant.

Bile rose in his throat. He thought he might vomit. What had the peaceful man done to warrant such cruelty?

At that moment, every guard in the yard stood at attention, and a hush came over the crowd. Pilate stepped out on the balcony. He looked tired and impatient.

He addressed the prisoner. "This is the second time we've met. Have you anything to say?"

Jesus said nothing.

"Do you not realize that I have the power to release you? I also have the power to send you to your death."

The Jewish council stood in front of the crowd. They likely had something to do with Jesus' arrest. They were probably responsible for it.

The High Priest, Caiaphas, spoke. "If you release this man, then you are no friend of Caesar!"

Pilate's eyes narrowed. Ebenezer knew Pilate already had troubles in Rome, and Herod was always a thorn in the governor's side. Pilate certainly didn't need any more trouble. This didn't bode well for Jesus.

Ceremoniously, Pilate walked to the edge of his balcony, and the soldiers pulled the shackled Jesus directly beneath him. "I find no fault with this man! But I leave the matter to you!" He gestured to the crowd.

Ebenezer watched as Pilate sat down on what was known as the judgment seat. He couldn't believe his ears when the mob shouted, "Crucify him! Crucify him!"

Twice more, Pilate questioned the crowd, each time receiving the same response.

"Each year, it is the custom of the governor to release one prisoner during the celebration of Passover. I offer you this choice. I give you Barabbas, or this man, Jesus. Who will it be?"

Ebenezer had heard of Barabbas. He was a thief and murderer. Surely the crowd would not let him go.

He was wrong.

"Give us Barabbas!"

Ebenezer couldn't comprehend the madness. His anger reached a level he had never known. He cried out for the angel, but it did no good. The nightmare was real, and the angel wasn't going to stop it. The shouts of the crowd surrounded him, the intensity of their mission deafened him, and Ebenezer was swept up in their frenzy. He couldn't escape, and the angel had disappeared.

He put his hands over his ears. He screamed, hoping that the angel could hear him. "You can take me anywhere, or do with me anything you want, but spare this man! He's innocent of any crime!"

All went silent. Though the crowd still waved their fists and continued to call for Jesus' blood, Ebenezer was only able to see the insanity. He was stone deaf.

The angel appeared, and though Ebenezer still could not see the messenger's face, he knew the heavenly being stared at him.

Not since the death of his beloved sister had he ever thought of anyone but himself.

Here in the courtyard, surrounded by people shouting for the death of an innocent man, Ebenezer was willing to trade places. He was willing to die so that another human being could live. He didn't pretend to understand Jesus' power or comprehend that he was the Messiah. Right now, all that mattered was that the feelings of anger and grief which had held Ebenezer's heart captive for so long were gone. The man in chains had saved his life. Now he was prepared to do the same for him.

He didn't wait for the angel. With a shaking hand, Ebenezer reached out, indicating he was ready to leave. He knew it was going to be painful, but he was prepared to face his future, regardless of the consequences. He understood now. His travels with the cloaked angel weren't about Jesus. They were about choices. He could either follow the rabbi, or continue on his own path of self destruction. It was up to him.

As the mist enveloped him, Ebenezer watched the guards drag and whip the teacher into walking on his own to the fate which he'd been sentenced.

★   ★   ★

Once clear of the mist, Ebenezer watched the soldiers tie Jesus' arms to the patibulum, the beam that fit into the groove of an upright post like the ones that were permanent fixtures on top of the hill outside of Jerusalem.

It brought back a memory still etched in Ebenezer's mind: the father and son working in the small carpenter's shop, creating a smooth plank out of the trunk of a tree. Now, Jesus was being nailed to one.

Ebenezer could only watch through the mob of people as the bleeding, weak man stumbled along the rocky, uneven road. It was hard to comprehend this was the same man who walked through peaceful olive groves, sharing wisdom with a handful of followers. A boy picked up a rock and threw it at Jesus. So different from the children who used to pick flowers and braid them into chains to place around his neck.

Ebenezer kept up with Jesus, trying to get as close to him as possible. It didn't matter if Jesus saw him or not. This was the man who'd started his life in Ebenezer's own stable. The innkeeper had turned a blind eye to the baby then, but he would not forsake the grown man now.

A woman ran up and spit on Jesus, her face made ugly by judgment and disgust. Ebenezer recalled the woman who was caught in adultery, and how lovely her face looked when she found forgiveness.

So many faces. So many lives saved. Where were those people now?

Jesus tripped, and Ebenezer instinctively reached to break his fall. Though no living soul saw it, the teacher looked at Ebenezer. He looked past the greed, the narcissism, the anger, the hate. He looked into Ebenezer's heart, and dissolved all the septic rancor that had filled it. In that one look, Jesus set him free.

Time stood still. He gazed into his teacher's eyes. His Savior's eyes. Ebenezer believed. He knew in that instant he was face to face with his Lord. Jesus was the Son of God.

With that, the two men—one invisible, the other visibly headed to His death—walked side by side up the hill to Golgotha, better known as Skull Hill.

Once they reached the top, Jesus turned to look at the innkeeper one last time. Ebenezer made no attempt to hide his tears.

"Why? Why are You doing this? You don't have to die! You can stop it. I know You can."

A soldier pushed Jesus toward the cross, and Ebenezer heard Christ's words: "For you. I'm doing it for you."

Ebenezer tried to comprehend Jesus' words. *What does that mean? Why does He think He needs to die for me?*

From this distance, Jerusalem sparkled in the sunlight. It was magnificent. A nauseating contrast to the scene behind him.

He heard the sounds of the spikes being driven into Jesus' wrists and ankles. He fought the visual agony of turning around, but his heart and mind wouldn't surrender. Slowly, he turned. They were nailing an innocent man to the crossbeam.

The crowd had dwindled. They had no problem encouraging the governor to sentence a man to such brutality and death. They just didn't want to have to watch it carried out.

The thought was sickening. He realized he'd done precisely the same thing. His decisions had sentenced others to a life of mental and emotional agony and financial ruin. It was easy, as long as he didn't have to see the consequences. Ebenezer was as guilty as the crowd who'd called for Christ's death. Ebenezer just never used a whip or nail.

There were so few people now standing around that it was easy to see everyone who remained. Where were all the followers who listened so intently to the teachings of the Man now hanging on the cross? Where were all those He'd healed? Where were all the men who were constantly in His company?

The only ones determined to see this gruesome public display to its inevitable end was a small group standing as close to the cross as the soldiers would allow. Several were women, and when the wind blew one woman's veil away from her face, Ebenezer saw it was Jesus' mother. He'd heard her cries of pain bringing her son into the world, and now he heard her cries as she watched Him die.

This was the second time Ebenezer watched a woman grieving the loss of her son. He couldn't fathom the sorrow and pain they must feel.

Though he knew it impossible, Ebenezer yearned to console the woman. He didn't know why, but he felt the need to support and protect her. Then it dawned on him. How could he have been so blind? She was his sister—not in the true sense, of course, but in the endearment she rekindled in his heart. He understood now. He was watching a woman who would, at that moment, gladly die if it meant her son would live. Years ago, his sister had.

Jesus spoke. They would be among His last words, yet they

were all Ebenezer needed to ultimately grasp the essence of the Man he'd followed since His birth. Even in death, Jesus asked God to forgive those who had sent Him to die.

Ebenezer couldn't bring himself to walk away, and the angel was nowhere in sight, so he sat and watched as the soldiers mocked the 'King of the Jews' and rolled dice for Jesus' clothing.

Even though it had been a sunny day, clouds began forming and thunder rumbled in the distance. The sky grew darker and darker.

'Appropriate,' he thought.

A bolt of lightning streaked across the sky. The wind began to howl.

Out of nowhere, the angel appeared at his side. Ebenezer reached out his hand. He no longer feared the angel or whatever lay ahead. He'd reached the point of acceptance.

"Angel, I feel as though our time together is short. There is no more you need show me. I have seen my Savior die. What more is there?"

The sky was encased in thick, black clouds. Just when mist began to enfold Ebenezer, the earth shook, and he saw Jesus take His last breath.

Seventeen

As the mist settled, Ebenezer was standing in a dark, stark field. There were no stars or moon to help him identify his surroundings. "Am I supposed to know this place?"

Ebenezer's voice was pensive, not challenging or demanding. The angel could take him anywhere, as far as he was concerned. It no longer mattered. His best friend was dead.

He turned around, taking in the landscape. He squinted. There was something out there. Boulders, maybe?

The angel held out its sleeve. Ebenezer touched it, not caring anymore about what it covered.

He was correct: What he'd seen in the distance were boulders. Now Ebenezer stood in front of one different from the other rock formations—and then he realized what it was. The enormous stone covered the entrance of a tomb. He heard a noise and stepped back. He thought pieces of the hillside were breaking loose and about to land on his head. But the noise wasn't from above. It was in front of him.

Slowly, the mammoth rock began to move. Even Samson would have struggled to push such a stone, yet by some invisible strength, it rolled away from the entrance. The angel pointed in the direction of the sepulcher. There were steps leading down to the belly of the grave.

"You want me to go in there? Why? What am I searching for here, among the dead?"

The angel remained silent and still. Its transparent hand continued to point toward the tomb.

Ebenezer shook as he crept down the stairs. He kept his back to the wall to keep from falling. Once he reached the bottom, the angel was already there. A soft, low light illuminated the crypt. From where it came, he didn't know.

The angel stood next to a shroud-covered body lying on a slab of stone. Ebenezer began to sweat, despite the coolness of the cave.

"Before I go any farther, answer me this. Are the things I've seen shadows of what *will* be or what *might* be? A man's actions lead to certain consequences. If those decisions change, so will the outcome. Isn't that true? I beg you. Answer me, please. Is this not true? Are you never to speak to me?"

The angel remained quiet, and pointed at the body.

"Tell me, angel. Am I the one lying there?"

The angel looked at the body, then back at Ebenezer. It continued to point.

"No! No!" Falling to his knees, Ebenezer tried to grab the black robe, but he felt nothing. "Please hear me. I'm not the man I was. I will not be that man again. Why show me these things if I'm beyond all hope?"

The angel was relentless in his silent demand.

Ebenezer sat back on his heels, resigned. "I've watched an innocent man crucified. Innocent children slaughtered. Mothers grieving for their dead sons. I guess nothing you show me now really matters."

He took a deep breath and stood next to the slab of stone. He reached over the body and pulled back the shroud. He thought himself prepared, but he wasn't. He felt the blood drain from his face. Ebenezer was ready to see himself on that cold stone, but not the face before him.

There, in what seemed peaceful sleep, was the Man whom Ebenezer loved. He fell back as he stared at Jesus. Recovering, he dropped to his knees. He was quiet for a moment, then said, "It should have been me. It should have been me."

Mist filled the room, but this time Ebenezer wasn't going anywhere. The angel began to disappear.

"I don't know if I can reverse my own fate, but please, please, let this man live! I beg you. I swear to you that I will always remember this night. I will not shut out the lessons you've taught me. But, if someone must die, let it be me. I know you have the power! Please." Ebenezer sobbed, and with his hands clasped, he begged.

The angel disappeared. Then came the scraping rumble of the large boulder rolling back and settling into place. The tomb was sealed.

Ebenezer sat next to Jesus' body. He couldn't stop the tears. He wept the long-pent-up tears of grief. Agonizing grief for the sister he lost. The one true source of his joy. And he wept for the loss of his friend. His Savior, who'd brought back the joy.

As his heaves subsided, Ebenezer realized he had no desire to go back to the living world. He belonged here, among the dead, for everything that was good, true, honest, and pure was in this room. He crawled to the wall and leaned against it, wrapping his arms around himself.

This is where I belong. Over the years I've become a wicked man. I've ceased to have any redeeming qualities. The angel was correct. They will celebrate my death. Yes. I deserve this.

His eyes grew heavy. Soon he slept.

★ ★ ★

Ebenezer slowly woke, a soft light shining in his eyes. He was disoriented, and the brighter the light grew, the harder it was to see. He shielded his eyes. The light bounced around the room, dancing up walls and across the ceiling. It finally came to rest in front of him.

"Gabriel? Is that you? Please speak to me. I feel so lost. I don't know what to do," Ebenezer babbled. "They killed Jesus. I don't know why, but they killed Him!"

Gabriel's face appeared in the light. Ebenezer tried standing, but his legs and feet were asleep, and he fell back against the stone wall.

"I never thought I'd see you again. I never thought I'd want to. But you are the only one who can help me."

Gabriel now stood in front of Ebenezer. "Help you with what? Please tell me, why are you sitting in this cold, empty tomb?"

"They crucified Jesus. They nailed the Son of God to a tree. Why, Gabriel? Please tell me so I can understand. Why did God let Him die? If someone has to die, it should be— Wait! What did you say?"

"I asked what you're doing sitting on the floor of an empty tomb?"

Ebenezer looked behind him. There was nothing but the pale, thin, stained shroud rumpled on top of the slab. "Someone has stolen the body!" He pulled himself up by leaning on the wall. "We must find it!"

"You plead for the life of a dead man, but where is He? There is no one here."

Ebenezer spun back to face the angel. "He was here. Where could they have taken Him? Gabriel, we must find Him!"

"No one has stolen the body."

Ebenezer was still confused. "Then where is He?" He banged his fist on the wall in frustration.

"He's risen, Ebenezer. Jesus lives."

The bewildered man slid down the wall, plopping on the floor like a rag doll. "I don't understand what you're talking about. He was lying right there. I saw Him. He was dead." He pointed with one hand, and held his head with the other. "Oh, what do I know? I'm not sure of anything anymore."

Gabriel's light softened. "You have witnessed the greatest miracle this world will ever know, Ebenezer."

He shook his head. "I don't understand."

"You offered your life for Him, but He's already given His life for you. He died so you might live, and now He lives so that all who believe in Him will never die."

Ebenezer looked up at Gabriel. "I mean no disrespect, but are you deliberately trying to confuse me?"

Gabriel began to float. "Jesus never wanted you to *die* for Him, Ebenezer. He wants you to *live* for Him! Look for me no more. Remember all that you've seen and heard this night. Take it to heart, and live the lessons you have learned. Live, Ebenezer! Live!"

Gabriel's light burned brighter, and he spread his wings. Ebenezer's breath caught in his throat. He'd never seen anything so beautiful. Gabriel smiled. Ebenezer reached out to touch the angel, but he disappeared.

The only thing Ebenezer touched were the blankets on his bed.

Eighteen

E benezer was on his knees in the middle of his bed. He tried to get his bearings. He had no sense of time. No clue what day it was. How long had he been gone? Had he really gone anywhere at all?

He cautiously rose out of bed and tiptoed to the outer room. The only light was the shaft of starlight coming through the window. He went into the courtyard and sat on the now-familiar bench. He leaned back and looked at the star. *Are you part of this story? Is there some reason you shine down on us?* He closed his eyes and let the breeze brush his face. He inhaled the sweet scent of flowers.

He remembered the small, childlike angel. The flowers it had draped around its neck. Was it real? Was any of it real?

He tried to recall the day at the inn, watching the crowds filling the rooms. He'd actually turned away the couple because they couldn't afford the cost. Ebenezer's heart pounded. Yes. He'd turned them away. Mary and Joseph. He knew that part wasn't a dream. He'd been ruthless and heartless. *Then, what does this mean? Are they in the stable at this moment? Has she had the baby?*

Then Ebenezer remembered Mary's screams. The knives.

He was overcome with remorse. Tears of shame trickled down his cheek.

"How could I have done that? Was I that cold and unfeeling?" More tears. He knew the answer was yes.

His actions weren't any better. He remembered berating Aaron. And, oh—Aaron's son. The crippled child. That poor, sweet child. "Oh, Timothy!" Ebenezer covered his heart with this hands. "I've been callous, cold, and—yes, I've been cruel."

And Isaac. How terrible I've been, mean and coldhearted toward the only family I have. He's right. My blood flows in him. My sister's blood. What heartache I've caused.

Ebenezer fell to his knees, and clasped his hands in front of him. "Whether real or dreamt, it doesn't matter. I'm a changed man. I will remember what I saw. I won't forget the lesson I've learned. And I'll always, always, serve my Savior. Jesus. Your seal is on my heart."

With overwhelming gratitude, Ebenezer walked inside. He began lighting lamps. Facing the condition of the room would only solidify his belief that he traveled with the angels. It was littered with broken pottery and spilled porridge. The fireplace tiles were dirty and silent. There was nothing that resembled the beautiful room he'd seen earlier. But it could, he thought. This house will be beautiful again.

Something caught his eye. His sister's bell sat on the table in front of the hearth. He remembered Gabriel knowing where it came from. He picked it up and held it to his heart. "Oh sister, how I wish I could share with you all that has happened. You would be overcome with happiness. You were such a giving, loving soul. I hope that, in the future, I will be more like you, to emulate your short life. I've wasted so much of mine."

Ebenezer had an idea. Which led to more ideas. He searched until he found what he needed and made a list. Not a ledger of numbers, deposits, or withdrawals, but a list of things he wanted to accomplish. It wasn't just a "try to accomplish, hope it happens" list, but a "living" list. Nothing could be crossed off until someone's life improved as a direct result. He wrote until the sun came up.

Even without a good night's rest, Ebenezer felt wide awake. He decided to get his plan underway. No time like the present. He had no idea what would happen, but he was prepared to do whatever necessary to help those whose lives he'd made so miserable.

As he walked into his room, he saw a flicker on the wall. Was Gabriel back? No, merely the candle flame reflecting in an old, grime-covered mirror hanging among cobwebs on the wall. Wiping the mirror clean, Ebenezer studied his reflection. His beard was long and scraggly, almost obliterating his face. What he saw was far from impressive. He looked the way he'd lived. Mean and hard. But there was something about his eyes. They didn't fit the rest of his face. They sparkled.

He found his razor, but remembered he had no water. He retrieved a jar to fill it, but found it already full. A small square of soap and a clean towel lay next to it.

His dirty clothes still lay in a heap in the corner, so the lady who worked for him hadn't been there. Who could have done it?

Ebenezer smiled. "If angels travel the world unseen, I'm sure it's no problem to fill a water jar!"

The razor was dull, but it did the job. Ebenezer stared at his face. He was surprised. He almost didn't recognize himself. He leaned closer. Where were the wrinkles between his eyes from all the years of scowling? They were gone. He once had lines around his lips from pursing them together. They had disappeared. Instead, when he smiled, a dimple appeared in the right corner of his mouth. The skin around his steely eyes crinkled when he smiled. His face was transformed. It matched his heart.

Bathed and dressed, he made his way to the courtyard. Repaired, it could be a beautiful place. A few flowers did their best to find the sunlight through the cracks of the broken stone. Walking through the gate, he noticed the broken mezuzah on the ground. He placed it back in the hole and made a mental note. The builders would replace it, as well as the one at the inn.

As he strolled through town, Ebenezer thought about the list he'd made. Much would change. Many would benefit. The thought made him ecstatic. He figured that's the way life was supposed to work. By helping others, one's own life improved. Memories of listening to Jesus' stories about such things flooded his heart. "I understand now. I'm just sorry it took so long."

Nineteen

The first place Ebenezer went was the market. People were preparing for another day of work. He recognized many of those he had seen packing their carts, now unloading their wares. He paid close attention to conversations to figure out what day it was. He was shocked to learn the angels had completed their mission in one night.

"They must have been in a hurry, for I have so much to do!"

Ebenezer greeted everyone with a smile. He was almost giddy as he strolled about, working on his plan. He was glad the registration was still going on—not because of what it did for his business, but for what it made available. There was access to products he wanted that would have otherwise required a trip to Jerusalem.

He saw the woman with her children beginning to unload their cart of bread. He bought several and paid her extra, "Since the loaves are so fresh." He went to stalls where he bought fruit, vegetables, and smoked fish. Beef was hard to come by, but when one found it, the price was so high, few could afford it. But Ebenezer saw a man trying his best to find someone who could. He paid the man his asking price, knowing it would help feed the vendor's family for several days.

Ebenezer bought a bolt of light green fabric. Very seldom did one see anything but brown. People might as well be wearing uniforms. He included new thread and needles.

He bought new books for the boys, and a new trough for the girls to kneed dough, but the best gift of all was carved from an olive branch and engraved with a name.

Ebenezer couldn't remember the last time he'd had so much fun. Strange, he always thought he was happy—the more money he made, the happier he became. Sometimes, he realized, greed and profit mask themselves, deceiving and conniving to make a person think they will bring happiness. They bury themselves in one's heart, gradually growing like a boil, until there's no room for anything else.

As he made his way through the market, he spoke to all the vendors and laughed at their jokes. It seemed nobody from the village recognized him. But why would they? Ebenezer had never paid them any attention. They probably thought he was a pleasant, wealthy man who'd come to Bethlehem to register and was buying gifts to take home to family.

Ebenezer decided he'd done enough for the time being. He needed to find a cart. He saw a boy cleaning out a stall. A small cart was propped against the wall. He greeted the child.

"Shalom, my dear boy. How are you this fine day? How would you like to make two shekels?"

The boy's eyes opened wide, a smile across his face. But then he looked doubtful. "What do I have to do?"

"Nothing sinister, I assure you. I would like for you to make a delivery. You see all these bundles? I need them to go to a particular house. I can't deliver them myself because I want it to be a surprise. Can you do this? I will pay you for your time. A shekel now, then another when you return."

"I must ask permission, first."

"Of course you do. I'll wait."

The boy disappeared. Ebenezer watched the crowd. He overheard bits of conversations. Lighthearted talks about family. Heartbreaking discussions about the census and taxes. He used to love talking about money and the different ways he could make more. Now he saw the other side. These people were suffering, barely getting by; in many cases, as a direct result of his greed.

The excited boy returned. "I can run your errand. But I have to hurry. My mother wants me to finish my chores."

"Then off you go! Here's the shekel." Ebenezer told him the family name and the street. "Remember, this is a surprise. No mention of who sent you."

"I promise."

Ebenezer walked on, heading toward the inn. He paid attention to every sight and sound. The angel was right. He'd never noticed his surroundings. He'd never paid attention to anything outside of his small sphere. He made mental notes of things to add to his list. He vowed to restore the community.

The opportunity presented itself almost immediately, when he noticed the two men who had come to the inn the previous day. Ebenezer greeted them, and it was obvious they didn't recognize him. When he introduced himself, they were surprised then guarded.

"Please let me apologize for my actions yesterday. I was offensive and rude. I realize that now. So, if I may, I would like to make it up to you. With a little planning, I believe we could make this an ongoing endeavor. If you would stop by the inn, we can discuss it further."

The men nodded but were still skeptical.

Ebenezer continued. "In the meantime, please accept my donation of—" He leaned over and whispered in the man's ear.

"Are you serious?"

"Quite serious. However, there is one stipulation. Please tell no one about our transaction. It is to remain anonymous."

Both men nodded.

"Now, I will be quite busy today, but may I count on seeing you tomorrow?"

The men said they would, and thanked the innkeeper profusely.

Ebenezer couldn't believe how content he felt. A sensation that was hard to describe.

Villagers greeted him as they would a stranger—as if he looked familiar, but nobody could place him.

He stopped by the small synagogue and prayed. Then he met with the rabbi, and they discussed what repairs needed to be made to the building. Construction meant jobs. Everyone would benefit..

★   ★   ★

There was one more stop to make before going to work. He stood outside the house, then he paced. Until now, making amends had been easy. This, was going to be difficult. He was going to come face to face with his past. How it went would decide his future. He finally knocked on the door. He touched the mezuzah and kissed the sacred symbol.

When his nephew opened the door, Ebenezer saw the surprise on his face.

"Uncle Ebenezer?"

"Shalom, Isaac. May I come in?"

"Yes, of course." Isaac stepped aside.

Ebenezer faced his nephew. "I won't take up much of your time, but I—" He cleared his throat. "I was wondering, if the invitation was still open, I would love to join you and your wife for the Sabbath."

Isaac stood with his mouth open.

"I realize this is a shock to you. Frankly, I'm a bit shocked myself. This is all very new to me."

Recovering, Isaac smiled.

Ebenezer almost wept at the resemblance to his sister. It was so obvious. His anger had kept him from noticing the boy at all. He couldn't see past his resentment. How could he have been so blind?

"Of course you're still invited! You are always welcome here!"

Isaac introduced his wife, who immediately tried to make Ebenezer at home.

"I'm afraid I can't stay, but know this—we will be seeing much of each other. We have much to discuss. Walk with me?"

His nephew followed him outside.

"Isaac, I have wasted so much time. I pray you will find it in your heart to forgive me for acting like such a fool. We are family. I'd forgotten how important that is. I have treated you in the worst possible way. You never knew your mother but, trust me, she would consider my actions detestable. She was an extraordinary woman. I would love to tell you about her. For instance—" Ebenezer swallowed. "Her favorite color was blue."

Isaac began to weep. Ebenezer pulled him into an embrace. Love seared through his heart, and he knew that he'd never be alone again.

Twenty

A short time later, Ebenezer arrived at the inn.

Noticing the broken mezuzah dangling from the door frame, he touched it, and the stone crumbled. "Don't worry. You will be fixed too."

Just as he'd hoped, Aaron had yet to arrive. Ebenezer dismissed the night watchman, assuring him they'd talk soon about expanding his working hours and responsibilities. Of course, more work meant more coins for his purse.

Ebenezer had never officially met the man. Aaron dealt with him. Before today, Ebenezer would have considered it beneath him. Now, he knew the night watchman's name, his family situation, and hopes for their future. Ebenezer promised he no longer needed to worry. The man left with tears in his eyes.

It was now time for Ebenezer to implement his plan.

He began doing all the chores Aaron was expected to do upon arriving. He straightened and wiped down furniture, cut every candle wick, and filled the lamps with oil. He collected fresh water from the well, and gave the jars to the women who cooked the meals. He thought one of the women was going to faint. He also asked them to pack small bundles of bread and cheese to be given to any guests preparing to travel home.

Ebenezer realized how hard his assistant worked. He'd never considered all Aaron had to accomplish every day. *And he had to do it while I stood looking over his shoulder, barking orders all day. What a fool I've been. A heartless fool. Well, that's about to change.*

★   ★   ★

When Aaron arrived, he didn't see Ebenezer. He was confused when he realized his chores were already completed. The day was getting stranger and stranger. First, a boy came to the door with a cartload of gifts. Nobody could figure out who sent them or why, and the boy refused to give them even a hint.

His family had never seen so much food, much less the selection. They would never have been able to buy such delicacies. Martha cried when she saw the bolt of fabric, and the children exclaimed with delight when they saw their gifts. Timothy's expressions and whoops of joy brought the entire family to tears. But who, they wondered, would do such an incredibly charitable act?

And now this? What was going on?

"Aaron!"

Well, that didn't take long. But no matter how angry Ebenezer was, or how badly he treated him, Aaron was not going to let the cantankerous man ruin the day.

"Aaron!"

Taking a deep breath, he went to stand across the table from Ebenezer, and averted his eyes.

"You are late. We're busier than we've ever been, and you come sauntering in here like you have all the time in the world.

144

You'd better have a good excuse!"

"I apologize." To say more would just be wasted breath. He still refused to look at Ebenezer. Seeing his scowl would interfere with the image he had of his family's joy.

"Do you have any sort of explanation? Something at home, perhaps? Is someone ill?"

Why does he care? Ebenezer had never asked about his life outside of the inn. If the man was going to fire him, Aaron might as well tell the truth.

"We had a delivery this morning, and it took some time to, uh, take care of it." He looked up—and then gaped at the innkeeper in astonishment.

"What's the matter? You look like you've seen a ghost!"

Aaron didn't move. He just stared at Ebenezer. Finally, he looked around the room. It was clean, organized, and filled with light. Normally it was dark and gloomy, and reeked of wine, sweat, and lamp oil. What was going on?

Aaron studied Ebenezer's face. It was his employer, yet it wasn't. Not only was the man freshly shaven and wearing clean clothes, but his face was different. Ebenezer was smiling.

★　✱　✱

It was time for Ebenezer to have a serious conversation with Aaron. The man appeared to be in shock. The innkeeper walked around the table and put his hands on his assistant's shoulders. "Don't worry. You haven't seen a ghost, and you're not dreaming. It's me, Aaron. It really is me. Here. Sit down. Get comfortable." Ebenezer gestured to the cushions. Then he poured a small

145

amount of wine and offered it to Aaron. "Just a few sips now. It's early. I thought you might need to calm your nerves."

Aaron just nodded, not taking his gaze off Ebenezer, and guzzled the wine.

Ebenezer laughed. Timothy was right. He'd forgotten how good it felt.

He sat down across from Aaron. "As you have probably surmised, something has happened. There's been a significant change."

Aaron nodded. "Yes. I can see that. But I don't understand."

Ebenezer smiled and shrugged. "I can't say I do, either. But for now, there is one thing of which I'm certain. I have wasted too much time blindly walking through life, believing the only thing that mattered, the only thing required for one to be happy, was how much money he had in his pocket. The truth is, I've never really known true happiness. I've had opportunities, but never pursued them. I guess I didn't think they were very lucrative. What a fool I've been."

Ebenezer took the empty cup from Aaron. "Starting right now, that's going to change. Today is a new day, my friend. The beginning of a new life." He saw the confusion and disbelief in his assistant's eyes. "Yes, Aaron. A new life for both of us."

Aaron remained still and quiet, watching and listening to Ebenezer talk. The innkeeper was excited about his ideas, enthusiastically gesturing as he listed his intentions.

"The first thing is, I'm increasing your wages. You have been severely underpaid and so I plan to make up for it. Second, I will be making repairs to the inn. The synagogue and my home as well. I will be asking Isaac to oversee these projects. You will help him when you are available. And if your sons are willing, and you agree, they may work in some capacity, and will, like everyone else, be financially compensated."

Ebenezer paused and looked at Aaron, trying to read his

face. "You look a little pale. May I get you something?"

Aaron shook his head. "I'm listening."

"It will be necessary to hire more help to take care of the inn. Once you're available, they will report to you. The inn will be yours to run."

"Why won't I be available? Where will I be?"

"With Timothy."

"I don't understand. How does my son fit in to all this?"

Ebenezer knelt in front of Aaron. "You will be helping Timothy. That will be your priority. I give you my word, Aaron. I will do whatever it takes, no matter the cost or how far we have to travel. With God's help, your son will be healed. You and Martha will take him to Jerusalem. Rome, if necessary. We will keep searching until we find the best physicians available. He will walk, Aaron. I believe it with all my heart. He will walk!"

Aaron began to sob. Ebenezer sat next to his kind assistant and embraced him like his own son until Aaron regained his composure. At first he wasn't sure he should, but his heart told him it was the right thing to do. It was the closest he'd ever come to being a father.

★ ✴ ✴

Aaron believed in miracles—he always had—but this was beyond his comprehension. His prayers had been answered. His son was finally going to get the medical attention he needed. But because of Ebenezer?

Aaron believed God answered all prayers. Sometimes the answer was no. Sometimes the answer was wait. That was the most difficult. People gave up, thinking God didn't hear them, but on those occasions when the answer was yes, they were surprised. Many thought it merely coincidence. They found it difficult to believe that God, the Almighty Jehovah, would actually answer their prayers. When He did, they were stunned.

That's exactly what Aaron was. Stunned.

He studied Ebenezer as he explained his plans. The man was giddy with anticipation. He couldn't wait to get started. The transformation was indisputable. He wasn't the same man who left the inn the day before. It wasn't just his appearance. There was something that had changed on the inside. His heart. Aaron could see it in his eyes. He was happy. He'd found peace.

But even in this new-found happiness, Aaron felt there was something troubling Ebenezer. He decided to be forthright and ask what it was.

"Ebenezer? What's wrong? I know you're concerned about something."

Aaron saw the hesitation. He could sense Ebenezer's apprehension.

He waited.

★　★　★

Ebenezer knew he had to say something. But how? What would Aaron think? It didn't matter. He had to address it. The sooner the better.

"Aaron, I know about the couple in the stable." He blurted it out. Not what he'd planned.

He watched the color drain from Aaron's face. He looked on the verge of panic.

"No, no. I'm not talking about where they are," Ebenezer reassured him. "Aaron, I—"

It dawned on him. Maybe Aaron didn't know who the couple was. Should he say anything until he was sure? He'd sound like a fool. Aaron would think it blasphemous. Ebenezer would have to take that chance.

"Aaron, I know *who* the baby is."

Ebenezer swallowed. His mouth felt full of sand. He couldn't imagine what Aaron was thinking.

"How?" Aaron's question was barely above a whisper.

"It really doesn't matter, does it? Not now anyway. Aaron, I am more ashamed of the way I treated them than you can possibly imagine. Please, don't ask me how I know, but what lies ahead of them is almost unspeakable. Events that no amount of trying or money can prevent."

Ebenezer's eyes became misty. He ached for the family. What they'd have to endure. The only comfort he had was what would happen in the end. *The fact that there really was no end.*

He searched Aaron's face for any sign of anger or disbelief. All he saw was compassion.

"We have much to discuss. But the first thing we need to do is find another place for the family to stay. I want to make sure they have everything they need."

"I'm sure we'll have a room later today. I will make sure it's ready. What else may I do?"

"Take care of our customers. I spoke with Isaac earlier. He will be here shortly to handle things for a while. I told him that you and I had business elsewhere."

"You mentioned earlier that Isaac would be helping with the construction projects. I'm surprised. But everything that's happened today has been a surprise."

"I know. Yesterday I'm cursing at him, and today I'm giving

him a job. As I said, we have much to discuss. But not now. We have things we need to do."

"You said we had business elsewhere. What is it, exactly?"

Ebenezer said, "Hurry and finish your responsibilities. Then I'll explain."

★ ★ ★

Aaron did hurry. He realized it was Ebenezer who'd completed many of his chores, so it didn't take long.

Isaac walked through the door just as he was finishing up. Both men acknowledged they had no idea what had caused Ebenezer's transformation, but agreed it was a miracle.

Ebenezer entered the room and greeted his nephew with a hug. Aaron shook his head. It was still inconceivable. If he wasn't seeing it, he'd never have believed it.

Ebenezer asked if Aaron was ready to go.

He assured him he was. He just had no idea where.

★ ★ ★

The two men walked into the sunshine, calling out greetings to those they passed as they made their way around the inn. They stood at the top of the hill, and Ebenezer turned to face Aaron.

"I have a favor to ask."

"What is it?"

"I want you to go down the hill with me. I want to go to the stable."

Aaron paused. "Are you sure?"

"I'm sure. I want to meet our guests." Ebenezer looked down the hill. He spoke so softly that Aaron almost missed it. "I want to see the baby. I want to see Jesus."

Aaron had no idea how Ebenezer could know such things, but something had clearly happened. Ebenezer was a different man. Timothy was right. It had been a night of miracles. And one of them was walking by his side.

Twenty One

Ebenezer scarcely believed the number of men, women, and children who had congregated around the stable. People from all walks of life were gathered at the entrance to the cave. There was little conversation. Even those who couldn't see into the cave seemed content to be close by.

As peaceful as it was, it was still a stable. And because of him, the Savior of the world was born here. Ebenezer was again filled with remorse. It was a disgrace. Would the world ever forgive him?

The reverent atmosphere quickly changed to one of scorn and contempt. There was malice in the people's eyes. As he made his way behind Aaron, the crowd parted like the Red Sea. Ebenezer knew that if they were not in this place, he would surely be mobbed. As it was, biting comments hissed through the crowd.

"Why have you brought him here?" Joseph walked out of the cave. He was obviously trying to stay calm, but Ebenezer could see the man's anger just below the surface. Ebenezer figured Joseph would like to berate him, repayment for the day before. He wouldn't discount physical harm, either. Instead, Joseph kept his voice low.

"Aaron, I trust you to do what's best for my family. Still— I don't understand why you've brought him here."

Aaron moved closer to Joseph. "Because this is why your son was sent here. He was born for people like Ebenezer. The lost, the hurting. He's come to save everyone, Joseph. And he won't pick and choose who that will be."

A hush went through the crowd. Emerging from the stable was the young mother. Mary walked past her husband, and gave Aaron a slight nod, but her focus was on Ebenezer. She looked into his eyes and held out her hand.

Slowly, he raised his shaking, sweaty one. Taking it, she turned to lead Ebenezer into the stable. She walked in front of him as they made their way through the thick hay. Ebenezer paused to let his eyes adjust to the light. He saw Timothy sitting in the corner with a lamb curled up in his lap. The child smiled at Ebenezer as though he'd been expecting him.

Against the wall was a stone trough full of fresh hay. Mary pulled back a small blanket, then moved out of the way. This gave Ebenezer a full view of the sleeping child.

The innkeeper thought he was ready for this moment, but nothing could have prepared him for this.

He knelt in the hay, clinging to the side of the manger. His gaze never left the child. Tears ran down his face. There was no gold. No silver. No chests of precious oils, or silks. But Ebenezer knew he was kneeling before the King. This was holy ground.

★　★　★

As he bowed his head, the transformation of 'Ebenezer the Miser' was complete. Ebenezer worshiped his Savior.

A Letter From Timothy

My friends,

I want to share with you what happened in the years that followed Ebenezer's redemption and transformation. I only wish you were there to witness it.

Ebenezer was a changed man. He became my father's best friend and a second father to me. He gave his family ring to Isaac, and had the official papers drawn up and signed, making Isaac Ebenezer's son and heir.

He kept every promise he made.

The inn became a favorite gathering place both for travelers and for those who lived nearby. It was known for having clean, comfortable rooms, good food, and exceptional wine. The prices were fair, so it seldom went without customers.

His home was restored to its original beauty, and was constantly filled with sounds of laughter and music. Friends and family were always welcome, and it became a favorite venue for Sabbath meals and celebrations.

Ebenezer had a never-ending list of projects; therefore, few men were ever without work. He helped repair homes or build new ones. Some were used as shelters for those trying to get back on their feet after Rome's greed left nothing to support themselves. He even added a wing to the synagogue for a small orphanage. He believed no child should ever feel abandoned.

Some laughed to see the change in Ebenezer. But he didn't care. He was a wise enough man to know that nothing good ever happens in this world that doesn't cause some to wonder about its origins or motives. Many thought him crazy, while others considered him blessed.

Father told me about Ebenezer's travels with the angels when I was old enough to understand. Well, as much as any other human can. Even Ebenezer was uncertain how or why it happened. But he wasn't bothered by it. The reason didn't matter. He was a better man for it.

It is said that if any man knew how to live the lessons Jesus taught, it was Ebenezer. When he died, people mourned. For those who loved him, the world became quieter. It wasn't until his passing that everyone realized how much joy he brought to their lives. They missed his contagious laughter.

As I said, Ebenezer was a man of his word, including those he spoke to my father that morning so long ago. One in particular.

Ebenezer lived long enough to see me walk. He never doubted I would. Remember the gift of the engraved olive branch? It was a staff to help a grown man maneuver as he walked long distances. It was engraved with my name.

Now, I plan to travel. Wherever the Lord leads, I will follow. I will spread His word.

That was my promise to Ebenezer.

I will leave you with the prayer I said as a child.

"God bless us, everyone!"

CPSIA information can be obtained at www.ICGtesting.com
Printed in the USA
BVOW04s1912071213

338477BV00005B/255/P